Start Your Own

BAR AND CLUB

Additional titles in *Entrepreneur's **Startup Series***

Start Your Own

Arts and Crafts Business

Bed & Breakfast

Business on eBay

Business Support Service

Car Wash

Child Care Service

Cleaning Service

Clothing Store

Coin-Operated Laundry

Consulting

e-Business

e-Learning Business

Event Planning Business

Executive Recruiting Service

Freight Brokerage Business

Gift Basket Service

Grant-Writing Business

Home Inspection Service

Import/Export Business

Information Consultant Business

Law Practice

Lawn Care Business

Mail Order Business

Medical Claims Billing Service

Personal Concierge Service

Personal Training Business

Pet-Sitting Business

Restaurant and Five Other Food Businesses

Self-Publishing Business

Seminar Production Business

Senior Services Business

Specialty Travel & Tour Business

Staffing Service

Successful Retail Business

Vending Business

Wedding Consultant Business

Wholesale Distribution Business

Entrepreneur
MAGAZINE'S

startup

3RD EDITION

Start Your Own

BAR AND
CLUB

Sports Bars › Nightclubs
Neighborhood Bars › Wine Bars
and More!

Entrepreneur Press and Liane Cassavoy

EP
Entrepreneur.
Press

Jere L. Calmes, Publisher
Managing Editor: Marla Markman
Cover Design: Beth Hansen-Winter
Production and Composition: Eliot House Productions

This publication is designed to provide accurate and authoritative information in regard
to the subject matter covered. It is sold with the understanding that the publisher is not
engaged in rendering legal, accounting, or other professional services. If legal advice or
other expert assistance is required, the services of a competent professional person
should be sought.

Library of Congress Cataloging-in-Publication Data
Cassavoy, Liane.
Start your own bar and club: sports bars, night clubs, neighborhood bars, wine bars and
more/by Entrepreneur Press and Liane Cassavoy.—3rd ed.
p. cm.
Rev. ed. of: Start your own bar and club/Sonya Shelton. 2nd ed., 2006.
ISBN-10: 1-59918-349-8 (alk. paper)
ISBN-13: 978-1-59918-349-7 (alk. paper)
1. Bars (Drinking establishments)—Management. 2. Taverns (Inns)—Management. I.
Shelton, Sonya. Start your own bar and club. II. Entrepreneur Press. III. Title.
TX950.7.S53 2009
647.95068'1—dc22   2009026605

Printed in Canada

13 12 11 10   10 9 8 7 6 5 4 3 2

Contents

▲

Preface

Opening a bar or nightclub sounds romantic. You might envision yours as *the* place to go in town. Many people fantasize about the idea, but few actually do it and even fewer make it successful. It's one of the more risky types of businesses to embark upon, so it's important to have a road map. This book was designed to provide one for you.

People go to bars and nightclubs for many different reasons, and as options for entertainment continue to grow, you have to make the choice to visit your bar or club compelling. It's not good enough to just have a selection of alcohol and open your doors. First, this book will explore the types of bars you might consider and give you some tips to flesh out your concept.

Next, you need to decide how to begin to build your dream—from the mission to the strategy to the structure to the people and processes. Every component is equally important. Many budding bar owners think they can approach the business as informally as the casual environment they want to create. This couldn't be farther from the truth. The bar and nightclub business is highly regulated and has a high rate of failure, so to be successful you need to have a solid plan in place right from the beginning.

Moving from idea to reality requires a great deal of research about the local market trends and your customer base. The questions you need to ask and the tools you need to do your market research and to scope out the competition are provided. (The latter part can be a great deal of fun, and it's part of the business!) You will also receive guidance around two of the most important factors: your bar's name and location.

As you start to get closer to the reality of your dream, you might also be overwhelmed by the amount of paperwork and regulations involved in opening a bar or nightclub. Federal, state, county, and local agencies have requirements and regulations for bar owners, and if you also provide food, it's even more daunting. Don't worry, this book will help you through the avalanche of paperwork and permits and show you how to shovel yourself out in a way that protects you and your business.

Next, it's time to design the layout and buy the equipment. From bar stools to beer taps, you have worksheets to help you decide what you'll need and how much to spend as you figure out your budget and startup inventory. Then, it's time to decide what systems and processes you'll use to prevent theft and ensure your success when the doors open. An entire chapter is devoted to one of your most important assets—your employees. They can make or break your business with the quality of their service, their knowledge, and their honesty. Ways to staff your bar or nightclub and the questions to ask before you hire are all discussed within these pages.

Finally, the focus is on two keys to success: marketing and entertainment. Entertainment options with and without performers are explored. Once everything is in its place, it's time to let the world know you're open. But marketing a bar is an ongoing part of staying in business, so some tips and tools to help you make a grand entrance and keep your customers coming back night after night are provided.

While it's vital to constantly remember that running a bar or nightclub is serious business, don't forget to have fun. You have the opportunity to express your own creativity with your bar and have a blast in the process. With the right amount of planning and dedication, you can make your bar or nightclub everything you imagine in your dreams and more. Best of luck in your adventure, and enjoy every moment!

1

Cheers! L'Chaim! Salud!
Industry Overview

Friends, laughter, celebrations, entertainment—fun! These are the things that might come to mind when you think about owning your own bar or nightclub, as you imagine rooms filled with friendly conversation, music, and people enjoying themselves. If you're thinking of opening a sports bar, you might envision an exciting game on flat-screen TVs with everyone cheering and having a great time. Owning a bar or nightclub sounds like the perfect life to many potential entrepreneurs, but it's not always fun and games behind the scenes.

Owning a bar/club can mean long hours, giving up vacations and weekends, and sometimes dealing with unruly customers. But if you have a clear vision, do your homework, and learn the ins and outs of the business, it can also translate into a rewarding and financially successful enterprise.

Bars aren't like retail establishments. People don't go there just to buy a drink or two and then leave. Depending on the type of bar or club you want to own, it will be a place where people can hang out with their friends and co-workers, negotiate a big business deal, celebrate a special occasion, and meet new people. People want to be around other people, and your bar can provide an excellent opportunity to fill that human desire.

A Look Back at History

According to the history books, people have enjoyed consuming alcohol for thousands of years. Ancient writings on clay tablets describe the use of wine and beer for religious ceremonies and rituals. That's a lot of alcohol consumed over 4,000 years! Back then, people fermented fruit juices into wine, honey into mead, and grain into beer. In some parts of the world, alcoholic beverages were considered safer to drink than water. Plus, alcohol could be stored in barrels, and it would still be safe to drink over long journeys.

In the Golden Age of Greece, establishments known as *phatnai* served traders, envoys, and government officials from a variety of regions. In fact, tavern growth generally followed the development of trade, travel, and industry all over the world.

The early American settlers brought the tradition of the English pub over the Atlantic Ocean and invented the American tavern. In 1634, the first tavern was opened in Boston by Samuel Cole. In New Amsterdam (later New York), Gov. Kieft grew tired of entertaining Dutch colonial guests in his own home, so he opened a tavern and lodge to accommodate them. That same building became New Amsterdam's first city hall and remained so until the current one was built in the 1880s.

Fun Fact

Way back when Rome controlled what is now England, alehouses were signified by a broom sticking out above the door. They were run by women known as alewives.

Back in those days, the government required every community to have some kind of public meeting place, and they usually ended up being the taverns. The government set regulations for their operation and controlled the prices.

People's interest in bars has long centered a great deal around television. First, it was to see the new invention. Then, they wanted to watch big-screen TVs, and satellite-broadcast programs from all around the world. Now, they want to see high-definition programming on big, flat-screen TVs that they may not be able to afford at home. You'll often see television reporters interviewing people at bars about the latest hot political topic or sporting event.

Although people still gather to socialize in bars just as they have for hundreds of years, other factors have come into play for the industry as well. Problems with driving while intoxicated have changed the drinking patterns of people in the United States. The growing concern with health and fitness toward the end of the 20th century took its toll on the bar industry. Keeping tabs on this industry requires a look at the alcoholic beverage industry as a whole—what people buy in the store doesn't differ much from what they buy in a bar. So what's the status of the modern alcoholic beverage industry?

According to the Distilled Spirits Council of the United States (DISCUS), "In 2007, distilled spirits grew for the eighth straight year, with sales up 5.6 percent, totaling $18.2 billion." The Council predicts that, despite a weakening economy, liquor sales will continue to increase, and consumers "will continue their fascination with cocktails and high-end products."

DISCUS chief economist David Ozgo notes that "spirits and wine increased their market share in 2007, while beer lost share for the sixth year in a row." While the troubled economy will certainly pose challenges to the liquor industry, Ozgo is confident that revenue will continue to grow.

There are more than 70,000 bars, nightclubs, and drinking establishments in the United States—and that figure doesn't include restaurants that serve alcohol. This means you have some pretty tough competition out there. But you're not just competing with the other bars in your area these days. You're competing with every entertainment option from which your customers can choose. And in a down economy, you're also competing with people's desire to stay home and save money. More than ever, you have to give them a reason to leave their homes.

Fun Fact

Many celebrated Americans throughout history owned taverns, including William Penn, Ethan Allen, John Adams, and Andrew Jackson. George Washington distilled whiskey, and Sam Adams brewed beer after the Revolutionary War. Abraham Lincoln also held a tavern license in Springfield, Illinois.

The Competition:
Other Entertainment Options

In the 21st century, the bar/club industry is more challenging than ever. The climate of entertainment began to change in the late 20th century. People have more and more entertainment options inside the home. These days, people not only have cable TV, but they also have the internet, which provides them with access to movies, music, and video whenever they want. According to Michael O'Harro, board member of the Oxford, Mississippi-based National Bar & Restaurant Management Association, as a bar owner, you should look beyond other bars for your competition.

"People never have to leave their houses," O'Harro explains. "You're not just competing with the bar down the street or the movie theaters. You're competing with people who are staying at home and entertaining themselves there. So you have to give them a reason to leave the house, especially in a down economy."

Stat Fact
The alcoholic beverage industry generates more than 3.8 million jobs and $78.6 billion in wages for U.S. workers. In addition, it's estimated that the distilled spirits industry annually contributes more than $100 billion to the U.S. economy.

Not only are you competing with your potential customers' urge to stay home and take the easiest—and cheapest—path to entertainment, but you're constantly trying to balance what your customers want with what you're able to give them. People's drinking habits change based on their needs and resources. But there will always be a need for a well-run, comfortable place to patronize. "Bars provide a place for people to interact socially, to meet other people," O'Harro says. "And that's just something that you can't get at home with a pizza and a movie."

If your goals include a wide variety of customers, and you are able to meet and exceed their expectations, then there's plenty of opportunity for you to fill up your establishment. According to The Gallup Poll, more than 62 percent of Americans consume alcoholic beverages. Good news is also on the horizon. Younger (but legal, of course) consumers have demonstrated an appreciation for drinking. They don't seem to drink as much as the generations before them, but those who do are more discriminating.

The popularity of higher-priced microbrews and top-shelf liquors continues to increase, which is great for you as a prospective bar owner!

What You Can Expect

Even in a down economy, most experts agree that successful new bars can be in the black within the first six to 12 months, and they can go on to recover their initial investment within three to five years. However, like many new businesses, the statistics for

To Bar or Not To Bar?

Just because you like to drink doesn't mean you're cut out to own a bar. It can be a lot of fun, but it's also a lot of work and involves many more hours than other types of businesses. We've put together ten questions you can ask yourself to see if you've got what it takes to own a bar or club. Take your time, and be sure to answer honestly!

1. Are you prepared to give up lazy weekends hanging around the house and vacations for at least the next year—possibly three years?
2. Can you handle going to work every day without the security of knowing what to expect when you get there?
3. Are you willing to risk your savings for your business?
4. Are you willing and able to work seven days a week and 12 or more hours a day, if necessary?
5. Are you willing to sacrifice your social life for the success of your bar?
6. Can you take on the responsibility of leading a staff and conquering obstacles when everyone else has given up?
7. Are you a late-night person?
8. Do you feel comfortable being the host of the party and striking up conversations with total strangers?
9. Are you comfortable dealing with large amounts of cash on a daily basis?
10. Can you say "no" to free drinks for your friends, relatives, business associates, and employees?

If you answered "no" to any of the above questions, you might want to think about it a little more before you open a bar. It's a rewarding business, but it's not for everyone. Some people just make better bar customers than bar owners, and it's important to find out early which category you fit into.

bars aren't in favor of the startup. Why do they fail? The first reason is they didn't have enough capital to keep the business going. The second reason is a lack of knowledge about the business. And in a tough economy, it's more important than ever that you do your homework prior to opening.

> **Stat Fact**
> According to the Washington, DC-based Beer Institute, the brewing industry provides more than 1.7 million jobs in the United States and generates $190 billion in U.S. economic activity annually.

Are we trying to scare you out of owning a bar? Maybe. If you're not interested in a high-risk business, this isn't the one for you. But if you look at risk as a challenge waiting to be conquered, then this may be the industry for you. If you're still not sure, check out "To Bar or Not to Bar?" on page 5 to see if you're really ready to give this business a shot.

From a personal perspective, you need to ask yourself if you're really the type of person who wants to own and run a bar. Of course, you don't have to run it if you own it, but you'd better make sure you have a team of good, trustworthy managers working for you if you plan to be "hands off." In the beginning, you'll probably have to be greatly involved whether you plan to be an active owner or not. If you're the kind of person who would rather deal with paperwork or sit in an office where you don't have to talk to people, this business isn't for you. You'll need to be out there talking to people and shaking hands. Getting to know your patrons, even if it's just to say "Hi," can go a long way for your customer service.

Another thing you should consider is the time commitment and hours of operation. If you're an early riser, you might not enjoy having to work until 3 or 4 A.M. at your bar. If you have a family, you need to discuss how owning a bar will affect them. Many days you will have to be at your bar from the time you wake up—say, around 10 or 11 A.M.—to the time you go to sleep—say, around 4 or 5 A.M. As you can see, this could take a toll on your family life. Eventually, you'll probably be able to have a saner schedule, once your managers and staff are well-trained, but it may take six months to a year to reach that point. If this could cause problems for you or your family, you may want to reconsider the idea of owning a bar.

If we haven't scared you away yet, and you're ready to go for the bottle-in-the-sky dream, read on. We've designed this book to give you the tools needed to succeed.

What's Your Bar Type?

Before you get started on the actual nuts and bolts of creating your dream bar, you have to decide what kind of establishment you'd like to own. Let's take a trip through the various kinds of bars—from neighborhood bar to large-scale club—and see which one is right for you. We'll also introduce you to a few of the owners and experts we interviewed for this book and the types of bars they own (or would own if they could start over).

Neighborhood Bar

You'll find neighborhood bars and pubs everywhere in the United States. You might have one around the corner from where you live or across the street from where you work. They're excellent meeting places for friends and business associates. Depending on where you live, there may just be one, or there may be lots of neighborhood bars.

If you own this kind of place, you can expect to know many of your regular customers. It's because of the friendly "home away from home" atmosphere that neighborhood bars are successful. Some of these pubs open as early as 6 A.M. (as long as local laws allow them to do so, of course!), and they sometimes close earlier than other bars—depending on the clientele. This type of bar is perfect for small-scale entertainment options such as darts, pool tables, video games, and jukeboxes.

If you're thinking of owning a neighborhood bar, you might consider starting out with a beer and wine license first, and then moving on to a liquor license later if the business warrants it. You may or may not want to have a kitchen or extensive food menu, again depending on your concept and your customers. Some neighborhood bars offer sandwiches for the lunch crowd and appetizers in the evening, but no dinners. This avoids the need for a restaurant license and cuts down on costs.

Across the country, this is probably the most common type of bar you'll find. There are many neighborhood bars out there, but you might find there's room for one more in your area. According to the experts we interviewed, the startup cost for this kind of bar ranges widely, depending on the size and concept, but mostly on location. You can buy an existing neighborhood bar in a small town for $20,000 or even less, or you can spend millions of dollars building a brand-new one in a big city. Not coincidentally, the amount of revenue these businesses produce varies greatly, depending on your bar's location and capacity.

A benefit of owning a neighborhood bar is that you can duplicate it in multiple locations, which multiplies your income as well. "The bars that make a lot of money are those that can replicate the project many times," says Bob Brenlin, owner of three neighborhood pubs in Seattle.

Sports Bar

Depending on the establishment's capacity, sports bars can be a specific version of the neighborhood bar, or they can take on a life as big as a club. You may have the latter in mind, but your market research may point to the former. It's important to do your homework!

Generally, sports bars offer some kind of menu options, such as burgers, pizza, sandwiches, and appetizers. Since the main attraction is sporting events, sports bars have televisions in view of every seat, sometimes all tuned to different channels. Audio and video technology comes into play, with some owners spending a large percentage of their revenue on keeping up with the latest in technology—from satellites to HDTVs. As with neighborhood bars, startup costs and revenue potential vary widely, depending on the size, concept, and location.

Bright Idea

During the earliest stages of deciding to go into the bar business, visit several different bars within your local area and in other cities, too. Carry a pocket notebook and write down at least three of your favorite things about each bar as well as three things you'd improve.

If Bob Johnson, a consultant who runs a school of bar management based in Clearwater, South Carolina, decided to open a new bar today, he says he would start a sports bar for both business and personal reasons. "I love anything to do with sports," says Johnson. "I love to see people in a bar cheering for a team in front of big-screen TVs."

He also says it is a good business because you have built-in events to use in your marketing throughout the year. "There's always something to promote, there's always something to do, and there's always an aura of excitement in the room," he explains. "To complement the TVs, you can have video games and sports-oriented games so people can entertain themselves and have fun with each other. They can do more than just sit there and drink. You have to offer your consumer more than just the drink. They're not going to sit there and drink if there's not something going on to captivate them."

Brewpub or Beer Bar

Studies have shown that although consumers are drinking less alcohol, their tastes are becoming more discriminating. As a result, microbrews are more and more popular. In a brewpub, you can brew your own beer right on the premises. In a beer bar, you can offer a large selection of different types of beer, including microbrews produced elsewhere. It's often easier to get a liquor license for a brewpub or beer bar than a full-scale liquor license, since you don't need a fully stocked liquor bar. Another benefit to owning a beer bar or brewpub is that men and younger adults drink beer more often than any other alcoholic beverage, which can translate into a profitable business for you.

Some brewpubs only sell their own beer options on tap (draft beer), with a few selections of bottled beer options, too. Since you are creating your own product in a brewpub, you also have the ability to control what you make and sell—from quality to quantity. The startup costs of a brewpub can be quite high—from $100,000 to more than $1 million—because of the brewing equipment you need to have. If you produce a popular beer, you have the opportunity to grow into a very successful operation.

Beer bars tend to have lower startup costs, in part because they may require a less expensive, fixed-price license from your state government. Beer and wine licenses can be much easier to obtain than liquor licenses. (See Chapter 5 for more information on licensing.) Beer bar startup costs range from about $20,000 to more than $100,000, depending on size and location. The revenue potential depends on the geographic location and drinking trends in the community. For example, a beer bar in Ohio may make much more money than if the same bar were located in certain neighborhoods in New York City, simply because of what the clientele likes to drink.

Specialty Bar

Specialty bars, which concentrate on one type of libation, from wine to martinis, or theme, like cigar bars, are gaining popularity. Although some specialty bars focus on only one drink category, there must be a wide variety available within the genre. Take martini bars: They've become very popular largely due to the variety they offer. The traditional martini still has a solid appeal if made with quality vodkas and gins, but other mixes, like sour apple martinis and Cosmopolitans, have expanded the martini-drinking base, especially among women. But even with their increased popularity, martinis are still looking up at wine.

Beyond the traditional glass or bottle with a nice dinner, for many, wine is the drink of choice. In fact, women and older adults order wine more often than any other alcoholic beverage. Wine bars offer guests the opportunity to taste a variety of different kinds of wine and the ability to learn more about their qualities.

Specialty bars may stay small and intimate in size and are located in more sophisticated neighborhoods. The costs and revenues you can expect to find when opening a specialty bar depend mostly on the type of product you serve and your location.

Research Can Be Fun!

One thing you probably already know about the bar industry is that you're in the business of fun! So you can have a blast while you're making decisions such as the type of bar you want to own, and what kind of concept you want it to have. Here are some research tips to help you make your decisions:

❍ *Visit as many of the bars in your community as you can.* (We don't suggest a bar crawl; you have to remember what you saw!) Write down what you like and what you don't like about each of them. Can you see yourself in this type of bar?

❍ *Break the bars up into categories.* Don't hop from a club to a neighborhood bar to a champagne bar. Make a list of the successful neighborhood bars in your area. Then check out each of them before you move on to the next category.

❍ *Don't waste your time and energy.* If you've spent time in a couple clubs and the loud music gives you a headache, don't bother checking out the rest on your list. If you know a particular type of bar isn't for you, move on to the next category.

❍ *Visualize.* Use your research to start developing your own ideas. Imagine what your bar would look and feel like in contrast to those you explore.

❍ *Keep an open mind.* Unless you already know exactly what kind of bar you want and what kind of concept it will have, don't prejudge anything. You may discover that you would like to own a brewpub instead of a club, or you might incorporate other categories into your initial ideas. This is the time to really have fun with your brainstorming!

Club

Like the neighborhood bar, clubs can take on a number of different personalities. You can open a small cocktail lounge with a jukebox or a tinkling piano in the corner. A medium-sized club might look like a neighborhood bar during the lunchtime hours, then spring to life with a popular band at night. Or if you have a big enough budget, your club might be a large dance club where the most fashionable people and hippest celebrities hang out every weekend.

Whichever path you take, you must be prepared to spend a great deal of time and money on promotion to create your "buzz." Clubs can make plenty of money if they're managed properly.

Most successful clubs draw on a city population of 500,000 or more. If you're in a small town or suburb, you may not have the customer base to open a large dance club. Market research is the key. (Read Chapter 3 for the scoop on market research.) Depending on the entertainment you offer, you can develop a group of regulars that keep coming back or a transient clientele that visits your club for a specific show but doesn't return for several months. Smaller clubs may charge a low cover or none at all, while larger venues can charge $20—or more—at the door.

Creating Your Concept

Once you've defined the type of bar you want to open, the next thing you need to figure out is your concept. Your concept will drive nearly every decision you make from here on—including your location, size, menu, décor, and startup costs. The most important thing to keep in mind is that you are not just in the bar business, you are in the entertainment business. Like any other type of entertainment business, you need to create an image.

A successful concept doesn't just focus on the type of entertainment you want to provide. It can be detected all the way down to the finest details. You can use your concept to stay focused on what your bar is all about. Plus, it will help your guests describe it to others and spread the word.

If you already have a general location in mind, you may need to work in reverse. This will require some research. You want to develop a concept that fits in with your location's market. Ron Newman, a bar and restaurant owner in Manhattan Beach, California, worked with his partner to develop a concept that would fit into a beach locale. They found their location first and then developed a fun, shark-themed sports bar. They wanted to create a casual social environment with good food and drinks at reasonable prices. Their original simple concept resulted in three additional locations over a period of just seven years!

In developing his concept, Newman kept the big picture in mind right from the start. He visualized the marketing, T-shirts, décor, and big-bucket drinks with sharks in them. "Location is everything," says Newman. "You could take our concept and put it two miles up the street, and [you would do less] business."

Once you've decided what kind of bar you want to open and you've developed some ideas on what kind of concept you want to have, you

> **Smart Tip**
> *Tip...*
>
> When you're deciding on your concept, don't limit yourself. Brainstorm the wildest ideas. You may even find that your concept crosses over to different categories of bars. You don't have to spend a ton of money to create a cool concept. Sometimes the simplest ideas are the best!

▲

can get started on the actual structure of the business. Do you want to form a corporation or a limited partnership? Should you take over an existing operation or start from scratch? What do you need to get started? We'll address these questions and many more in the next chapter. So let's get going!

Deciding to Open
How Committed Do You Need to Be?

Now that you've decided what kind of bar you want to open and started developing concept ideas, it's time to think about your personal devotion to your bar. Opening your own business can be as much of a commitment as a marriage or having a baby. Your dedication and your experience will largely determine how much time you'll put into your bar once it's up and running.

In this chapter, we'll explore that commitment and help you refine your goals. We'll also go into the structure of your business, the professionals you need on your side, and how to come up with a mission statement.

But first things first. Before you start sorting out the details, you need to have a solid understanding of how much you want to commit to your operation. You do have options. As we briefly discussed in Chapter 1, not every bar owner works all day every day once the bar is up and running. R.C. Colvin, owner of Round Table Bar & Grill in Niles, Michigan, has structured his bar so the daily operations go through him. He's in charge. Whereas Gerry Kelly, marketing director of The Fifth in Miami's South Beach area, favors a hierarchical style of management. When he owned The State, a nightclub in South Beach that he recently sold, Kelly and his partner, Greg, had managers below them who ran the club while they worked the marketing end of the business. You can choose to go either way or find your own level of commitment somewhere in between.

All the experts we interviewed say you need some kind of experience in the bar or restaurant industry.

"There's so much to know about the bar business. If you don't have the right kind of experience, it could cost you thousands of dollars in mistakes," says Ron Newman, the sports bar owner in Manhattan Beach, California. "Learn on someone else's money."

Your experience will come in handy when you need to step behind the bar and take over when a bartender doesn't show up for work on time or when they're overwhelmed with an unexpected rush of business. If you have a little experience with basic accounting, you'll better understand your financial position when you look over your books. If you have enough working capital, you can pay people to do everything for you, but you should make sure they're competent, dedicated, and trustworthy. After all, you're putting the success of your business in their hands!

> ### Smart Tip
> Tip...
>
> When should a potential bar owner recruit a team of professionals—a lawyer and accountant familiar with the bar industry? "As soon as you think you might get into the business," according to Michael O'Harro, a board member of the National Bar & Restaurant Management Association. These experts can help you every step of the way.

On the Path to Ownership

In Chapter 1, you were introduced to your first two major choices: what kind of drinking establishment you want to run and what concept you'll bring to the marketplace. Your next two decisions will help you visualize your approach to starting your operation and determine what type of ownership your business will have.

You already know what you want out of this endeavor, whether it's as simple as money or as specific as giving people a place to drink and congregate. Earlier, you read about the different kinds of bars and hopefully fixed on one particular type that best suits your goals. You also learned the importance of having an overall concept for your bar and started brainstorming your own concept. Now you have to decide whether you want to take over an existing bar, start from scratch, rebuild a site, or invest in a franchise opportunity.

Obviously, if you choose to purchase an existing bar (that at least somewhat fits your concept, or that you think you could run better), you can begin to recoup your investment immediately. But you may also find yourself in the thick of real problems you didn't even suspect. On the other hand, if you choose to build from scratch so every little detail is exactly how you want it from the beginning, you may not make your money back for quite some time. Buying a franchise offers another option, where you can adopt someone else's established concept. This may require a bigger investment up front, but you're investing that money into work that someone else has already done for you.

When it comes to your knowledge of the bar industry, don't fool yourself into believing you can learn all you'll need to know as you go along. Although you'll learn new things every day, you should start with a working knowledge of the bar and nightclub industry; in addition, you'll need to know how to manage people, money, recordkeeping, and the quality of your products.

It's important to develop your team of professionals right away. An accountant will help you immensely when the time comes to help figure out your startup costs, financing, and working capital. Your lawyer can help you protect your interests and keep you out of trouble with licensing and regulations.

Another professional you may want to hire up front is a marketing specialist, says Michael O'Harro of the National Bar & Restaurant Management Association. "In today's economy, it's especially important to sell yourself and your concept." If you have a background in marketing, you may not need to hire outside help. But if you don't know the first thing about promoting yourself and your business, you'll need help right away, O'Harro says.

Think of all your hired professionals as members of your bar's team, and remember to use them as expert resources. Make sure they're capable and willing to step up to the plate. And make sure they have experience in the bar or nightclub industry. Find out if they've had other clients in the industry. Ask them if they've dealt with the complexities you'll have to face. You may be learning on the job, but you don't necessarily want the same to be true of your hired team.

Buying an Existing Bar: Patience or Profits?

By the time you're ready to decide whether you want to buy an existing bar, you should have a good idea why you're getting into this business in the first place. Just because you know of a good deal on a bar doesn't mean you're the right person to own it. You need to make sure it matches your goals and personality. And buying an existing bar isn't always a step-by-step process.

For example, you might walk into a sports bar named "Victor's," see the walls are lined with memorabilia from assorted professional sports teams, and think to yourself "This is the kind of place I want." You can't just walk up to the owner and tell him you want to buy it. He might not want to sell, and you may offend him. If you want to start your own bar, that particular bar may give you a point of reference to guide you through your development. On the other hand, your timing may be perfect. You can always talk to the owner and take his temperature if you want to slowly pursue the idea. Keep in mind that you might be taking over someone else's headaches. It's critical that you fully investigate the bar before you make any commitments.

Do Some Digging

If you're thinking about buying an existing bar, you want to accumulate as much information as you can. Get all the dirt on the place you're thinking of taking over. Here are some ways to go about that:

- *Become a regular customer.* Posing as just another customer in the bar gives you a great advantage in gathering truthful information about how it's run. If you sit at the bar, you can strike up conversations with other guests to find out their impressions of the place.

- *Ask specific questions to fine tune your perception of the operation.* Do you see the employees working together as a team? Are the bartenders only paying attention to their customers at the bar, or are they also attentive to their servers' needs? What are the customers saying about the atmosphere, service, and food?

Are the drinks consistent? Is the facility clean? Are the bathrooms well-stocked and clean? Do you like the décor? Do the details of the bar—from attitude to atmosphere—project the overall concept?

- *Make sure it's a good investment.* Generally, a fair price for a bar equals the amount of one year's gross receipts, but that can vary greatly depending on the location and other factors, such as the seller's motivation and the overall state of the economy. Check with your lawyer or accountant to find out if the offer is a good one. (Local business brokers and bar suppliers can also give you some great advice.) You can also compare the bar's inventory to the actual sales volume to make sure you're getting the right numbers for a year's gross receipts.

- *Conduct a complete inventory before and after you buy an establishment.* You want to make sure you're getting everything stated in your contract before you take over.

Building Your Own Dream

Ah, the excitement of closing your eyes and imagining exactly what your place will look like! You see yourself standing proudly behind the glistening bar and smiling. Then, you open your eyes and see the vacant lot your real estate agent has brought you to check out. Starting your business from scratch can be a long and expensive process. Its greatest return is how well it can match what you imagine. The old adage states that owning a business is like raising a child. Therefore, if you choose to build your bar from the ground up, in essence, you're genetically engineering your operation.

In addition to your accountant and lawyer, you need to enlist the services of an architect, contractor, real estate agent, and perhaps a banker (if you could use some extra financing help). These experts will help you establish checks and balances so your project doesn't spin out of control.

For example, say you bought a piece of land for your dream club next to an undeveloped area being purchased at twice what you paid. This will increase the value of your land—but you might find that the contractors' bids for your building go far beyond your budget because of this. You may find that it's wiser to sell your land for a profit and set up shop at another location that fits your budget. Your team of professionals should clue you in on things like this so you don't waste time and money.

Smart Tip

Tip...

If you're going to build your bar from scratch, budget every financial detail with high estimates. Plan your projected income with conservative estimates. Then balance these numbers against your resources before you break ground.

Remodeling: The Middle Ground

You may have visited many different bars similar to the kind of bar you would like to own. Perhaps you've taken a ton of notes, talked to a number of people, and found a bar owner who wants to sell. The place is perfect for you, except maybe you think the fireplace should be on the opposite side of the restaurant (or be gone altogether). You might think the kitchen should have a little more space, and you would choose completely different bar stools and chairs.

This happens to potential owners on a regular basis. However, it's not a good idea to try to make it all happen at once when you take over the business. If you want to remodel or drastically change the operation before you begin running the business, then you should add these expenses to your startup budget. Experts warn against a radical takeover and transition while operating under the same name. The regular customers and employees of the bar you've taken over could easily feel threatened and drastically affect the income you counted on when you bought the bar.

If you've discovered a place that has the potential to become what you want from your bar with a few renovations, you need to prepare your plan and make some decisions. First, analyze the changes that need to be made. Can they happen over time, or will you have to close your doors to make it work? If you have to close and reopen, you may want to consider a name change followed by a grand opening. This way, your team of professionals won't base your projected income on how well or how poorly the business has done in the past, but on what your projected operation will generate.

If you find a bar for sale that's very similar to the type of establishment you want to run, you may be able to make changes slowly, while keeping it open. You can simply emphasize the things you like about it and make the changes slowly. For example, you may find a location with a great outdoor deck, but the current owner rarely uses it. You could spruce up the deck and throw a summer kickoff party—say, for Cinco de Mayo—where you highlight several different kinds of specialty margaritas.

To decide whether you should purchase an operation that matches most of your ideas for your business, pull out a piece of paper and a pencil. First, make a list of what you want to change. Then, schedule a meeting with your team of professionals (that's your lawyer, accountant, and suppliers, remember?) and discuss the feasibility of the items on your list. You may not be able to make some alterations, like drastic changes in the kitchen, without shutting down for a little while.

Before making a final decision, you should weigh all your options. Should you close down

> **Fun Fact**
> In ancient Babylonia (around 1750 BC), the Code of Hammurabi stated that a beer proprietor who was caught diluting his ale could be put to death.

the old place and reopen it under a new name? Should you take over the operation of the business and change it over time? Or should you just wait for a prospect that better matches your concept?

Buying a Franchise: The Package Deal

It may surprise you to find bars that are franchise operations (as opposed to chains), but they do exist. Most operate with full kitchens, not limiting themselves to serving only appetizers and quick meals.

The same rule that applies to any other type of operation also applies to franchises: Knowledge of the industry is key. Joining a franchise gives you the chance to avoid some of the mistakes that could kill a fledgling operation (you'll be part of a larger, experienced organization). It may prove to be a good avenue for you to gain needed experience while you're running your own business.

Strap on the Weight or Divide It

Here's some insight into how the structures affect bar ownership. Most bars are structured as either a corporation or a limited partnership, depending on the ownership situation. Experts warn against structuring a bar as a sole proprietorship because of the personal liability involved if something goes wrong with the business.

Are you the type of person who only sees yourself when you're visualizing your bar? Did you save your hard-earned money to create your dream? Do you like to make all the decisions yourself, or would you rather work with a partner or a team? The answers to these questions will help you make your decision about the type of ownership you want for your bar.

Your team of professionals will undoubtedly make suggestions concerning the right type of ownership for you. Learn about your ownership options, and ask your team to clear up anything you don't understand. It's important you're confident in your business structure.

> **Tip...**
>
> ## Smart Tip
> LLC stands for "limited liability company." It's a favorite structure for bar owners of all kinds. Unlike a limited partnership, the limited partners in an LLC can involve themselves in the operating decisions of the bar. Be sure to use specific language in your partnership agreement detailing roles and responsibilities. Your attorney and your accountant can help investigate LLCs and other ownership structures.

19

An Open Invitation

When you take on partners, general or limited, you can put yourself in the middle of a whole lot of stress. It could get so bad that you start to pull all your hair out! Bob Johnson of the Clearwater, South Carolina, School of Bar Management offers the following advice on ownership structure and how to use it as a special weapon against failure.

"If you're going to have partners, the best way is to have a limited partnership. You might enlist 15 to 20 investors at $20,000 apiece. Then, what you've established is a nut of hard-core regulars. Those investors are definitely going to go by their place two or three times a week—not to boss people around, because only the general partner (you, in this case) would be allowed to actually operate the business," Johnson advises.

"When I go out looking for investors, I'm going out for professional people. On my 'dream team,' I'd have a lawyer, a CPA, a market researcher, and a promotions expert," says Johnson. "So if I have some problems, and we have to do something because business isn't quite happening or we're in a slump, I have these professionals at my disposal because they're my investors."

The line gets a little fuzzy between some ownership structures, such as a limited partnership vs. a limited liability company. In a limited partnership, there's at least one general partner and one—or more—limited partners. The general partner can be held personally liable, which makes this a risky proposition for bar owners. In an LLC, the owners are shielded from the debts, obligations, and liabilities of the company.

The best rule of thumb when drafting any of your business agreements is to get it all in writing. And remember to listen closely to your accountant and attorney when it comes to developing any kind of partnership agreement. "It should all be understood upfront: Everybody pays—no free rides," advises Bob Johnson of the School of Bar Management in Clearwater, South Carolina. "That's all part of the agreement, signed by everyone. Nobody can go in there and flaunt their authority. If they do, they take the chance of getting thrown out of the partnership."

Developing Your Own Mission

Perhaps because many hospitality operations have issued mission statements that largely resemble employee regulations, the mission statement has gotten a bad rap.

Your mission statement should simply state what you want to accomplish with your endeavor. It's not how quickly you greet guests when they walk in the door. It's not merely your décor or liquor selection. It's the reason you're opening a bar in the first place and why you think your bar will be successful.

Sometimes your mission statement can reflect what you don't want. For example, Bob Brenlin, a pub owner in Seattle, says, "I don't want to run a hard-drinking bar. You have drunken problems all the time if you do that." The "drunken problems" Brenlin refers to include issues ranging from belligerent treatment of employees by customers to having to clean up vomit every night. So Brenlin's mission statement is based on his desire to run a small bar/restaurant where people come to eat and to drink, but not drink exclusively. As a result, Brenlin's Seattle bar offers soups, salads, sandwiches, and the like to attract the kind of customers he wants for his operation. "Our particular business plan revolves around being a great pub," says Brenlin. "That's what we're all about: consistently offering a good quality product and service in a small neighborhood pub." Use the "Mission Statement Worksheet" on page 22 to craft the vision of your own bar.

Creating Your Business Plan

Bar owners face some specific issues when it comes to creating the right business plan. Most of the people who will be reading your plan won't be familiar with the bar or nightclub industry, and they may have negative connotations of it. The details of starting a bar can be extensive, and you want your potential investor or loan officer to be able to navigate through all the information quickly. You also want to create a stellar business plan that will convince lenders your new bar won't flop like 8 out of 10 do in their first year.

Most owners use a business plan to get financing, but it can also help you plan and develop your bar, too. If you envision it like a flow chart in a computer program, your business plan will signal challenges for you to solve long before they threaten your success. It's extremely important that you make a comprehensive plan. Even if you can afford to finance 100 percent of the project in cash, you'll be better off writing down all your expectations, projected expenses, market strategies, and so on.

Bright Idea

To give your business plan a professional appearance, make sure it has a table of contents. You also should start your page numbers over with each chapter. For example, Chapter 1 is numbered 1.1, 1.2, 1.3; Chapter 2 is 2.1, 2.2, 2.3; and so on. This way, you can expand, modify and update your business plan without having to renumber the whole thing.

▲

Mission Statement Worksheet

Although you'll find most bars don't have a written mission statement, the owners keep an idea of their bar's mission in mind. It's always a good idea to write it down so you and your management staff can refer to it to make sure you stay on track. As you develop your mission statement, be sure to answer the following questions:

1. Where do you want your business to be in two years? Five years? Ten years?

   _____

   _____

   _____

2. What do you want your customers to think of when they go to or talk about your bar?

   _____

   _____

   _____

3. Where do you fit in your community at large?

   _____

   _____

   _____

4. What are your responsibilities to your community?

   _____

   _____

   _____

Use the area below to synthesize your mission statement into a sentence or two.

Mission statement for: _____
                                        (your bar's name)

_____

_____

_____

The Best-Laid Plans

Your business plan will be your bible for starting your bar. You may continue to refer to it well after you open your doors, too. Here are a few tips to get you started on the first draft of your plan:

- ○ *Concept.* Remember you're not just opening another sports bar or the like. You're opening a drinking establishment with a particular personality that's an attraction to your target clientele. Specifically communicating why your bar will be unique in the marketplace may go a long way with lenders.
- ○ *Profit and loss analysis.* Include a cost vs. value section to represent your bar's profitability.
- ○ *Location.* Highlight the benefits of the location you've chosen, whether it's low-cost rent or high visibility.
- ○ *Staff.* Present as much detail as you can about the number of employees you plan to hire and how much you'll spend on payroll. You can even include sample schedules to help demonstrate your understanding of this expense and how you came up with your numbers.
- ○ *Risk-awareness.* Don't pretend that your business venture is a sure thing. You won't fool anyone, except maybe yourself, and your business plan will end up lopsided.

To give you an example of why business plans are so important, one bar owner who had enough money to finance his bar didn't think he needed to create a business plan. Since he didn't put everything down on paper in one comprehensive plan, he ended up facing some obstacles that resulted in a drastic change.

This young, marketing-minded bar owner had put his faith in an experienced manager to run the operation. The manager's strengths were in customer service, rather than behind-the-scenes management of money and inventory. These "back office" skills would have been detailed in a good business plan. The young

> **Tip...**
>
> ## Smart Tip
>
> There's a difference between a mission statement and a business plan. A business plan details what you're going to do, how you're going to run a successful business, and how much it's going to cost. A mission statement tells why you're going to run a successful business.

owner suffered through three or four other managers before he decided on paying a seasoned management company to take over his club. Luckily, he caught the problem just in time and managed to save his business from failure.

Now you should have an idea of how you would like to structure your business. You're on your way to developing a solid business plan, and you have your lawyer and your accountant at your side. In the next chapter, we'll try to figure out what type of people you want to attract to your bar based on your market research. This will help you refine your location options and add to the development of your bar's concept.

Who Are Your
Customers?

One of the keys to starting any kind of business is knowing your market and, more specifically, your potential customers. Before you begin implementing your concept with the type of bar you chose in Chapter 1, you have to make sure it will fit in with the trends and personality of your area. You might have the best idea in the world for your concept, but if it doesn't fit in with what your customers want, you're not going to make it.

Gerry Kelly, the club marketing director in Miami's South Beach, has achieved great success by recognizing the trends in the night-life industry, which are often cyclical. "It reminds me of fashion, where 'retro' is in, then it's out, then ten years later it comes back in," he says. "With night life, I think it's the same thing." In the mid- to late 1990s, when the economy was booming and lots of people were flush with cash, thanks to the dotcom market, Kelly operated a 44,000-square-foot mega-club. Then, after September 11, the U.S. economy went downhill, and tourism dipped. Kelly saw the effect this would have on the club industry and downsized to a more intimate 12,000-square-foot club called State. After about five years, he sold State and now works as the marketing director for The Fifth, another South Beach nightclub. South Beach is a lot like the nightclub industry as a whole, he says: It's an ever-changing city.

Tip...

Smart Tip

When you go to your local library to gather information, start with your friendly librarians in the reference department. They often know exactly where to find the information you're looking for so you don't have to spend hours pouring over books and articles.

Wherever your bar or nightclub is located, you need to do your homework to find out who your customers are and what they like. With some startup businesses, you can simply conduct surveys and research demographics. However, in the bar business, it's not so easy. You need to do a great deal of footwork (or hire someone to do it for you) to make sure you're on the right track. You may end up completely redesigning your concept around what you discover about your market.

Profiling Your Customers

The FBI has a department called the Behavioral Sciences Unit that creates profiles of criminals to help track them down. As a bar owner, you need to embark on the same kind of relentless detective work to profile your customers before you start investing large sums of money in your business. The majority of the research material you need is probably already available to you. You simply have to compile it. You can go about developing your customer profile in several different ways, then compare the results to determine your direction.

- *General demographics.* Contact your local chamber of commerce or the SBA to find out about the age, gender, income level, marital status, and political and religious affiliations of your target market. Your bar's concept may go in a totally different direction if you're in a college town with a high percentage of young, single students than if you're in a quiet, conservative suburb populated with families.

- *Local laws and regulations.* Remember the movie *Footloose*, about a town where dancing was outlawed? You wouldn't want to open a dance club there. Footloose was only a movie, but many cities and towns have their own laws that can be similarly quirky—and unfriendly to bar business. One town in Massachusetts, for example, doesn't allow patrons to stand while drinking beverages. That means that every bar customer must be seated. This cuts back on the number of customers in a bar—and if it's your bar, it will cut back on your profits, too.

- *Alcohol trends.* National and regional alcohol suppliers keep records of how their product fits into the market. Your potential suppliers can provide valuable information about your customers and what they like to drink. Generally, they're glad to help. If you do your research and have a successful bar, your suppliers will profit, too.

Demographics Detective

You can approach the market for your bar in one of two ways. You can open a bar in a particular area because you live there. Or you can develop a concept and then try to find a market where it can thrive. Either way, you want to make sure your bar matches the demographics and trends of the location. If you can gather information about your potential customers ahead of time, then you can customize your theme and products to meet their preferences. Demographics can give you a general overview of the local population. Here are ten questions you need to ask to get started on your demographic research:

1. What's the total population?
2. What percentage of the population is male? Female?
3. What's the average age range?
4. How many are married? How many have children?
5. What's the average income level?
6. How much of the average income is considered disposable income?
7. What's the average education level?
8. How much time and money do they spend on entertainment, and where do they go?
9. How much do area residents travel out of the area?
10. How many people visit the area from out of town?

- *Other important statistics*. Visit your local public or university library. Many libraries have business departments that have a wealth of information about demographics, income levels, and spending trends.

- *Lifestyle trends*. Call the lifestyle and entertainment editors at your local newspaper and regional magazines, as well as the advertising and marketing departments of local radio stations. They can give you information about your competitors and tell you more about the establishments that have been successful in the area.

- *Your customers and the competition*. You can discover a ton of information about your customers using internet resources. Besides general demographics, you can surf the web for information about other bars in the area. Read local blogs and gossip columns to find out where the action is and which bars are the hot spots. (This is especially important for clubs!)

Beware!

If you're taking over an existing bar, that doesn't mean you can skip the market research—especially if you're planning to make any changes. You may find out the current customers don't like your new ideas, and you'll end up losing money. If you're planning to keep the same name and concept, conduct a survey of regular customers to find out how they'll respond to your plans.

Scope Out Your Competition

One of the best indicators about your market will come from visiting other bars in the area. You can glean valuable information from a customer's point of view: Strike up conversations with other customers to find out why they visit that particular bar, as well as some of their likes and dislikes.

Bright Idea

According to Bob Johnson of the School of Bar Management in Clearwater, South Carolina, the best time to check out how your competition is really doing is on Monday, Tuesday, and Wednesday. "Most bars are making it on Friday and Saturday unless they have a special during the week," says Johnson.

You can also learn about pricing and menu options by watching the buying habits of your competitors' customers. Servers and bartenders can give you feedback on the people in the area and their experiences with them. You may also be surprised to discover how willing many managers and owners are to talk to you about their businesses. Most of the bar owners we interviewed gained much of their market research information by talking to other owners in the area about their experiences. Use the "Market Research Competition Questionnaire" on page 30 to help you gather the same kind of information on each of the competitors you visit.

"You can tell a lot about your market by spending some time in the area," says Ron Newman, the sports bar owner in Manhattan Beach, California. "Once you decide that you like a particular area, spend time there. Go out at night. Talk to different people. Hang out and find out what's going on. That's the best way to research the bar business."

Market Research Companies

If you have the budget, you can hire a market research company to help you gather information. The right company will have the tools and resources to give you a thorough background on your customer base. Market research companies can conduct focus groups and market surveys to give you a feasibility study and a clear picture of your potential clientele. They may come back to you with information that tells you it's the wrong area for the kind of bar you want to open and advise you on some other locations to consider.

Since it's their job to know what's going on in their area, market research companies can also give the inside scoop on other kinds of business developments. For example, you may find out that a large hotel, shopping center, or condominium complex will be opening in an undeveloped area. You could capitalize on that information by being the first bar to open there. You might even time your grand opening with theirs for additional publicity. Without insider information from your market research company, you might not have found out about the new development until it was too late.

However, market research companies cost money. You have to decide the best way to spend your investment capital. If you have the time to do the research yourself, you can use the money you would spend on a market research company for other developments.

With your competition research in hand, you may consider using a competitive strategy to establish your own bar. Here are a few of your options:

- *Cost-based market penetration strategy.* Many new bars use this strategy, but it's not always the right choice. Basically, it involves establishing your business by underpricing your competition. If you choose this strategy, you have to be careful with your expenses. It's best to have cost-cutting policies in place from the very beginning.

- *Differentiation strategy.* An ideal choice for bar owners, this strategy uses techniques to set your business apart from the competition. You can really be creative with

> **Beware!**
> Don't just open up the phone book to find a market research company. You want to make sure you get the right company to help you research the feasibility of your bar business. Ask restaurant and bar associations, other bar owners, consultants, and your local chamber of commerce for referrals.

Market Research Competition Questionnaire

When you visit the competing bars in your area, you want to use the information you gather to develop a competitive strategy for your own establishment. Improve on their strengths and capitalize on their weaknesses. Fill out this questionnaire for each of the bars you visit to help you assess your competition and your customers.

1. What type of bar is it? _____

2. What is the concept/theme? _____

3. Does the bar offer a full bar, beer and wine, or just beer? _____

4. Did you have to wait to be seated? How long? _____

5. How long did it take to get served? _____

6. What kind of décor does the bar have? _____

7. Is the bar clean? _____

8. Is the layout of the bar and tables efficient? _____

9. Does the bar serve food? _____

10. If so, what types of food does it have on the menu? _____

11. Does the menu offer enough variety? _____

Market Research Competition Questionnaire, continued

12. How would you rate the quality of the drinks? _____

   _____

13. How would you rate the quality of the food? _____

   _____

14. Does the cost match the quality/quantity of the food and drinks served?

   _____

15. How do you feel about the bar's atmosphere? _____

   _____

16. How is the service? _____

   _____

17. What promotions and sales techniques do you notice? _____

   _____

18. What feedback did you receive from the bartender/waitstaff? _____

   _____

19. What information did you get from the customers? _____

   _____

20. List three ways you would improve the bar.

   1. _____

      _____

   2. _____

      _____

   3. _____

      _____

this one! You may choose to focus on quality, atmosphere, menu or music—anything that makes you unique.

- *Concentration strategy.* This strategy focuses on a specific clientele. For example, if you were starting a martini and cigar bar, you wouldn't necessarily market to the general population. You might narrow your target to high-income clientele. You can choose to limit your market to a particular group or geographic location or base it on your specific type of service.

Using Your Research Effectively

Once you have compiled all your research, you can devise a concrete profile of your clientele. For example, you may decide your target customers are professionals between the ages of 30 and 50 who have incomes of more than $40,000 and like jazz music. Whatever you set as your target market will affect all the decisions you make from here on, so make sure you get it right!

Once you have your profile, you can develop your menu and bar inventory based on what your customers like. Look for trade magazines and industry associations that provide data on food and beverage spending patterns. The National Restaurant Association compiles annual statistics that detail the performance of many eating and drinking establishments across the country. You can get a large chunk of this information from your suppliers as well.

Keep in mind that you may have more than one profile to work with. You may have a conservative professional clientele during the daytime and a rowdy college crowd at night. If you use your research wisely, you can develop a bar that caters to both profiles for even more business.

Ron Newman caters to different demographics at his Southern California sports bars. In the afternoon and early evening, he has a more family-oriented clientele. (The kids love his shark theme!) Says Newman, "We have a slogan here: 'Let your kids run wild . . . they fit in with the rest of the customers!' The parents will come in Sunday evening after a day at the park or after a soccer game or whatever. The parents can sit and talk to friends. Meanwhile, you see 60 or 70 kids running around yelling and screaming." Later in the evening, Newman turns up the music for his nighttime clientele—singles and couples between the ages of 21 and 35.

Tip...

Smart Tip

You can find more information about ways to conduct market research, including a cost-analysis worksheet of primary research methods and sample surveys, in *The Market Research Toolbox: A Concise Guide for Beginners* (Sage Publications) by Edward F. McQuarrie.

Housing Your Dream:
Location

Once you've completed your market research and defined your potential customers, you can begin finding the perfect location for your dream bar or tavern. In this chapter, we'll lead you through the process of finding the right location for your business and then picking a perfect name that matches your overall concept. You may even end up with a name that relates to your location!

Your choice of location will depend on how you want your bar to look, what you want your bar to contribute to the community, and the kind of clientele you want to patronize it. Then you need to decide whether you want to buy the location or sign a lease. Again, that depends on your budget. Finally, you need to figure out how to fuse your concept with both your name and your location to your best advantage. So grab a map, and let's dive right in!

Unearthing the Right Location

Do you want to see a bar expert or consultant take off on an emotive dissertation? Just mention the word "location." People who know this industry well have polar opinions on the concept of location. Some owners and experts we talked to put enormous importance on the bar's location while others refuted its significance altogether. It all depends on what you want your bar to be and what your strengths are as an owner. If you want your bar to get impulsive neighborhood traffic in a particular area, then your location should be close and obvious. If you would rather spend the time and money saved by more affordable real estate to develop your establishment's concept and create your own buzz and destination, your actual location won't matter so much.

You should also consider factors such as safety, parking, accessibility to customers—even the history of the site—when choosing a location.

Your Bar: The Place to Be

Michael O'Harro, a National Bar & Restaurant Management Association board member, explains how he took a bar location nobody wanted in Virginia and made it work. "It was in an alley," he says. "It was a 15-foot-wide alley, and we were 128 feet away from the street. No one would go up the alley—[people] were afraid of it. So the building sat empty for 50 years. But the bar at the end of the alley was spending $20,000 a month in rent, while my rent was $500. I figured I had $19,500 to put toward marketing per month. I made the alley fun and chic. In the alley, I put down Astroturf that I purchased from a football stadium. I had signs, lights, and banners. It became "the" alley. Nobody knew it was there, and then all of a sudden it was the hottest alley in town."

On the other hand, you can have an incredible spot and still not be successful. For example, if you're lucky enough to have the only sports bar that's right outside your town's athletic stadium, you should be rolling in cash—at least during every in-season homestand. But if your staff is stealing from you, operating procedures are

Dollar Stretcher

Many landlords charge less rent for facilities on the sunny side of the street. Reasons for this include costs to cool the inside and difficulties involved in using a patio because of relentless sun. You could rent on the sun-soaked side of the street and use an awning or patio umbrellas decorated to communicate your theme as a form of free advertising.

badly managed, or your service isn't up to par, you could quickly find yourself out of business—grade-A location and all.

In general, a bar's location offers both strengths and challenges to you, the owner, and you should know what you're getting into before you sign on the dotted line.

Your first stop in searching for a location should be your local zoning commission. There may very well be zones within your target area where the sale of alcohol is prohibited. Don't get your heart set on a "perfect" site only to find out that no bar can locate there.

Also, you can get quite a bit of important information from your local beer, wine, and liquor wholesalers. They have a front-row seat to the drinking habits and alcohol distribution patterns in their areas. Plus, they'll be glad to help you for the opportunity to land your business once you're ready to open. Just make sure to do your homework and find wholesalers you can trust. You want to make sure you're turning to the best possible sources for information.

The Space Case

How much space you need to successfully run your drinking establishment depends on what kind of bar you open (club, pub, tavern, brewpub, etc.). You should also consider your earning expectations and whether or not you want to serve food. If you plan to serve food, you need to think about what kind and how much room you'll need to prepare it quickly.

Unfortunately, you'll constantly run into questions to which you can only guess the answers. For example, a common challenge is storage space. You may think you'll go through much less wine on a busy Saturday night than you actually do. Will your bartender have to run down two hallways and fiddle with two different keys and locks just to get backup wine bottles?

If the space you're considering is now a bar, then you'll probably have an easier time figuring out whether or not it's the right size for what you have in mind. If the facility you have your eye on is not now, and has never been, a bar or restaurant, then make specific plans and try to visualize what the busiest scenarios would look like. Pull out your pencil and paper and draw out a rough idea of what you want and how it will fit into a particular location you're considering. It's probably best to err on the side of too much space, especially in the kitchen area, but every bar has a different purpose.

Some general space guidelines are as follows:

- For a smaller pub, like a neighborhood bar, look for something in the range of 1,000 to 1,500 square feet.
- For a larger pub, like a tavern-style operation, you'll probably want up to 1,800 or even 2,000 square feet.
- Sports bars and clubs range widely, depending on how many pool tables and dartboards you want and/or how big you want your dance floor to be. A good ratio to shoot for is to have 25 to 30 percent of your overall space earmarked for live entertainment and/or dancing. So look for a site big enough to accommodate what you want to do, which could be 2,500 to 5,000 feet.

> **Fun Fact**
>
> Many years ago, people in the industry called beer bars—establishments that serve only beer—"brewpubs." Today, big and small breweries are adding quaint eateries that showcase their own beer, which is often brewed on the premises, but that doesn't make them brewpubs. A brewpub is only a microbrewery that incorporates a pub or an eating establishment.

Remember, you may not be able to begin your operation at the grand scale you want to achieve if you don't have room in your budget. If this is the case, make sure you have a space that allows potential room to grow.

Inside, Outside, Upside Down

By now, you have a pretty good idea of what you want your bar to be and who your ideal customers are. You also have a concept in mind for what niche you'll fill in the community. It's best to have all this written down in as much detail as possible so that when your choice of location starts to cause you to move your target, you'll know it right away. For example, if you're planning to use a sun deck, but you're considering a location that doesn't currently have a deck, you'll either have to factor in the cost of remodeling or refigure your plans.

Be objective and take your time. A big mistake commonly made by budding entrepreneurs is rushing into things at speeds way above the successful limit. Rushing usually happens when choosing a location and signing a lease. People often look past the potential problems, even those staring them in the face, because they get too excited and become blinded by their dreams. It's difficult to be objective when picking a place to make your own because it's your own personal vision that makes you want to open a bar in the first place.

This is why it's so important to write everything down and to get as many opinions as possible. You'll probably be able to convince yourself that you can turn any sow's ear into silk, even if you don't realize you're doing it. Throughout the course of your operation, you'll be able to get away with a lot of mistakes, learn from them, and become stronger because of it. But if you put the money you've budgeted into opening a location that won't fit your concept until you invest another large chunk of money, chances are you will not make it long enough to see your concept come to life.

Thematically Speaking

You may be asking yourself, "Why does this book keep harping on my concept?" Simply speaking, your bar's concept, or theme, will produce adjectives for your most important advertising—word-of-mouth. For example, if you've chosen rainbows as your theme, your bar may have very colorful decorations, and you might offer special drinks of every color in the rainbow. Your patrons will tell their friends about the cool purple drink they had, which will bring you more business.

This is why it's important to keep your theme at the forefront of your mind as you pick a location. If you find a place that's very dark but cheap, you'll have to find some way to brighten it for the rainbow concept to work. Or you can wait until you find a well-lit, airy place.

> **Tip...**
>
> **Smart Tip**
> Use your market research to focus on the type of area where you're most likely to find the clientele you want. Your location may fall into two or more of the following: business district, industrial center, residential, mall/shopping center, highway access, recreational (local parks), or entertainment district. Consider how your clientele will perceive the area and capitalize on that.

Please, Sir, May I?

Once you've located the right place for your bar and established what changes you want to make (or devised plans for a brand-new facility), you'll have to secure permission from the government agencies who oversee construction and remodeling projects in your community. Your lawyer will help you during these early stages.

Whether you're building from scratch or remodeling, you'll need to visit the building and safety department right away. By going to them before you begin, you'll save yourself the money, time, and stress of redoing the project to meet their standards and regulations. You'll also receive a preliminary occupancy rating, which may later be lowered by the fire department. Your occupancy rating will come into play when you start designing your layout (discussed in Chapter 6).

Most specifications for construction can be found in the Uniform Building Code, but local rules also apply. Be sure to get a copy of the regulations in your area from your local building and safety inspector.

Should You Lease or Should You Buy?

The primary advantage of owning the building that houses your bar vs. renting is the friendliness of your landlord. Buying the building has some disadvantages, including the upfront costs, the difficulty of obtaining a mortgage in today's market, and the possible long-term commitment—especially if the value of the property doesn't rise over time. As a property owner, you're in the real estate business as well as the bar business. And today's real estate market is a tricky place.

Beware!
Renting space in a shopping mall, plaza, or strip mall has become the latest craze. These places sometimes charge you a percentage of your profits over and above your rent payments. They also often add other charges in addition to rent for promotions and upkeep of the shopping center.

Because a lease is a specific agreement between the lessee and the lessor, every lease has different arrangements. Because of this, the advantages and disadvantages vary depending on the location you've chosen and the deal you and your team of professionals have hammered out.

You may have noticed we've been saying "it depends" on almost every topic related to finances and space. You'll probably see it quite a bit more throughout the book. Your bar will be defined by your own ideas, concepts, business practices, and the way it's perceived by its patrons: Everything about it depends on you. Every bar attempts to facilitate the happiness of its patrons, so bar owners offer what they believe will make the people they want to be their regular customers happy.

As a result, your bar's location and any modifications you want to make to it will be different depending on your community, your budget, the type of bar you want, your customers, etc. However, the more specific you make your goals, and the more detailed your plans are to reach those goals, the clearer the picture will become of what you want to achieve. Then it will be even easier to find out how much space you need and how much you should expect to spend.

A Bar by Any Other Name

When it comes to naming a bar, experts generally fall into two major schools of thought. The first says your bar is your dream—your hard work—so you should name

▲

Leasing Dos and Don'ts

As with any contract, you should enter your lease agreement with care and caution. Here are some things you should consider when you're getting ready to sign your lease:

○ *Don't act alone.* Enlist the help of a good attorney and a commercial real estate agent familiar with the area when negotiating a lease.

○ *Do talk to other tenants.* Find out what kind of caretaker your future landlord is by asking current tenants what they think. This will be easy in strip malls and the like, but you may have to follow up with references to make contact with previous tenants.

○ *Do read the fine print.* Your lawyer may assume you're on board with everything and not question fine points you don't like about the lease.

○ *Don't assume something is covered, like who changes faulty light fixtures.* Ask questions.

○ *Be ready to negotiate.* Don't assume you have to accept the landlord's first offer. Chances are, there's room to negotiate.

Michael O'Harro, a board member of the National Bar and Restaurant Management Association in Oxford, Mississippi, explains that negotiating your lease is a step-by-step process. "First, you have to find a building," says O'Harro. "Then you have to get your lease. Then you have to tear it apart, and make a better deal."

it anything you want. The second approach to naming says your moniker is the first and greatest form of advertising for your drinking establishment—and you should take advantage of that.

A name like Bill's Bar & Tavern doesn't really tell the public anything about your business, but The Haystack, Romp, and 3rd & Vine give customers something to connect you to. You wouldn't consider going to a bar called Romp if you just wanted a quiet drink. Likewise, you wouldn't travel up and down 4th Street looking for a place called 3rd & Vine.

Michael O'Harro of the National Bar & Restaurant Management Association in Oxford, Mississippi, advises that your name should exemplify your concept. "First, I would try to figure out what my concept is going to be," he says. "Sports bar? Discothèque? High energy? Low energy? Singles bar? What exactly am I going to be? Then, what's the name of this business going to be? I would do tremendous research to try to come up with a name that literally fit with the concept."

The name of your bar or nightclub can be more than just advertising; it also can have a subliminal effect, O'Harro says. "My sports bar was called Champions. I could have named it the Sports Pub, but Champions is a word that means something, something successful," he says. "I had a new wave club called Scandals and a disco named Tramps. Those names did the same thing: They created an effect."

What Was that Place Called?

When coming up with different names, don't stop until you love at least three. In your brainstorming sessions, keep these three questions in mind:

1. How well does the name fit the concept you want to create?

2. What types of customers will the name attract?

3. What will people expect based on the name?

If you already have ideas about your menu or have started thinking about your drink specials, they can help give you hints on a name, too. Sometimes when you come up with a concept, everything else just starts to fall into place. Can you come up with a name that promotes your unique products? For example, you wouldn't want to call your bar "Margarita's" if you specialize in martinis or single-malt scotch. Likewise, you should think twice before calling a brewpub that serves pizza "Jose's"—even if your name is Jose. Your name can be a calling card only if it fits your business. Use the "Name-Storming Worksheet" on the next page to help you come up with the best name for your business.

> **Smart Tip** *Tip...*
>
> When it comes to creating your name, theme, and concept, follow the two rules of brainstorming. The first rule: When you focus on a particular topic and work at it, great ideas will come. The second rule: Keep the focus on your goal rather than yourself. Remember, have fun!

> **Bright Idea**
>
> You may want to plan a trip to your Secretary of State's office to fill out the necessary forms and pay the required fees. But before you jump in your car, jump online. Most government offices have websites that list information about the process or requirements. This way, you'll know everything you need to take with you before you go.

Making It Legal

Registering a business name can be easy or difficult. It depends on how many markets you want to compete in and how unique your name really is. If you want to open one location in your community, you can get all the necessary information from your friendly Secretary of State's office in your state capital. If you want to open multiple locations in various states (or

Name-Storming Worksheet

This worksheet will help get you started on the name game. Your answers on this worksheet will give you a selection of adjectives and nouns that you can then turn into a name. Answer the questions in many different ways until you have at least three names that hit home with your entrepreneurial spirit. You don't have to stop with the list you develop here. Keep going until you run out of ideas!

1. Name three things you want to see in your bar:

   1. _____

   2. _____

   3. _____

2. List three adjectives that describe your concept:

   1. _____

   2. _____

   3. _____

3. What do you want your patrons to say about your bar?

   _____

4. What might be your customers' favorite books, songs, or movies?

   _____

5. What wild animals would be most at home in your bar?

   _____

6. What locales reflect your concept?

   _____

7. What historic events exemplify your concept?

   _____

8. Name three unique sights or sounds a customer might find in your bar:

   1. _____

   2. _____

   3. _____

even if you plan to eventually), or if you plan to sell merchandise on the internet under one name, then you'll need to do more research, and you'll likely need to hire a trademark attorney. This may make your naming process a little more difficult, but don't worry.

The following examples will give you a good idea of the range of difficulty you can expect while trying to procure a name for your establishment.

- *Easy scenario.* You're opening a neighborhood pub with a tropical theme in your state's capital. You don't have any plans to sell T-shirts or beer mugs over the internet with your name on them. All you have to do is go to the Secretary of State's office, make sure your desired name hasn't been taken by another bar in the neighborhood, fill out the appropriate forms with the names you want, and pay a fee. You need to have three names you would be happy with and rank them in order of preference. You'll receive the most preferred name on your list that hasn't already been reserved.

- *Difficult scenario.* You want a specific name for your place, and you've already designed a logo, emblem, and slogan based on that name. You've created your concept and menus in perfect sync with your perfect name. You know you want to copyright the name.

Then your trademark attorney tells you that a small bar on the other side of the country already has that name. Even though the other bar owner may never bother you about the naming rights, you probably don't want to count on it. You could be halfway into unrolling a big campaign and then run into trouble over your name. In this case, it would be best to rethink your name and go with one you can own solely.

You also want to do as much research into a name—using any government and online resources you can find—to make sure it's not taken. You don't want to waste a lot of time and money creating logos and merchandise only to find out that the name you want is unavailable.

The National Bar and Restaurant Management Association's Michael O'Harro agrees that you should have an eye toward the future when you're considering a name, and he says you need to protect your name as soon as possible. "If it's called Mike's Bar, you can't sell it to Bill," says O'Harro. "I've always considered myself creative, and I've tried to find names that would have a national appeal. As soon as I came up with a name, I copyrighted

Bright Idea
Go back to school! Don't worry . . . you don't have to stay very long. Many colleges have Small Business Development Centers that offer access to information about trademarks, financing, marketing, and a host of different subjects of interest to you.

and trademarked it, which a lot of tavern owners would never think of doing. I always felt that I was going to be so successful that other people would try to copy it."

Putting It All Together

Deciding which comes first—your bar's name or your bar's theme—is a lot like the chicken or the egg dilemma. In the end, it doesn't really matter. One comes from the other, which comes from the other, etc. They should be truly integrated. For example, what if you opened the 69th St. Alehouse, established it as one of the best pubs in your community, and then lost your lease and had to move three blocks away to 72nd Street? Would you change your name? It's been proved that naming your bar based on its location is an advantage when it comes to marketing and promotion. If you went into this undertaking constantly having to keep in mind what would happen if you had to move the whole operation, you'd probably drive yourself nuts. Still, it's a possibility.

When you hear the word "concept" or "theme," you may think of a high school dance committee your friend convinced you to join. However, we're not talking about crepe paper and silly string when it comes to running a drinking establishment. Your bar's concept is a large part of what gets customers to walk through the door. Underlying marketing messages like great beer prices, excellent DJs, and hip crowds will play a secondary role.

Whether or not you decide to concern yourself with promotions or the image of your business is up to you. However, you're still making these underlying marketing promises to your potential customers, whether you want to control them or not. If you resolve not to have any kind of special theme in your bar, that will come across. Maybe your community needs a simple bar with a plain atmosphere where people can meet for drinks, but your longevity may be at risk of being squashed by competitors and other available entertainment options.

With your location in place and your name picked out, we can continue through the process of opening your bar. You've officially signed on, and you're ready and excited to begin your journey as a bar owner. In the following chapter, we'll wade through all the paperwork involved in getting your business up and running. We'll go through all the steps of getting your licenses, permits, and financing so you can start moving into your new place!

5

Climbing a Mountain of Paperwork

In Chapter 1, we talked about the bar business being a people business. But when you're starting out, it's more like a lawyer's or accountant's business. Mountains of paperwork and lists of laws and regulations go along with opening a bar, including those concerning licenses, taxes, worker safety, liability, sexual harassment, and insurance.

Getting to the summit of all that bureaucracy may seem daunting. Take a deep breath. You have several resources you can tap to push you up the steep parts.

In this chapter, we'll start out with the paperwork you need to file, laws you need to follow, and your responsibility to your community. From there, we'll dive right into the money you'll need and some financing opportunities to get you started in your business. (That's right, more paper . . . but we like this kind!)

Remember your professional team from Chapter 2? Now is the time to keep them really busy. Your lawyer can help you wade through all the bureaucracy and laws, while your accountant will play a large role in getting together your paperwork for taxes, startup costs, and financing. You should also enlist the services of an insurance agent to help you make sure you meet all the insurance regulations for your area. So put on your hiking boots, and let's climb that mountain.

May I See Your License, Please?

As a business owner, you need to file for some standard business licenses and permits. You should also find out about the tax forms you need to fill out before you get started.

Before you do anything else, you should obtain an Employer Identification Number (EIN) from the IRS. This number will be required for many of your licenses and permits, and all your tax documents. The IRS even has a paper-free option for obtaining an EIN. You can go to www.irs.gov and, after answering a few questions, you can obtain an EIN online. If you'd rather do it the old-fashioned way, you can fill out IRS Form SS-4, *Application for Employer Identification Number*. You'll find the form on pages 48 and 49. After it's complete, you can fax it or mail it to the IRS.

As a bar owner, you have lots of permits and licenses to contend with at every level—from federal to local. This is a highly regulated business. The two most important agencies you'll be dealing with are the Alcohol and Tobacco Tax and Trade Bureau (TTB) and your local Department of Alcoholic Beverage Control (ABC agency). Let's start at the local level.

State, County, and Local Requirements

You'll find that bars face different requirements depending on where they're located.

Smart Tip *Tip...*
Be sure you understand all the state and local liquor laws before you start any remodeling or construction work on your bar. Some Alcoholic Beverage Control agencies have layout and lighting standards you must abide by. You don't want to have to remodel again before you open because you didn't understand the regulations!

Some states, counties, and cities have very complex laws and regulations, while others are fairly simple. However, all states require a liquor license to sell any kind of alcoholic beverage. In addition, the government dictates what you can sell, where you can sell it, when, and to whom. Some states even have regulations for advertising and promotion. In other words, the mountain of paperwork you climb varies in altitude and cost depending on your location.

The first place to start at the state level is your Alcoholic Beverage Control (ABC) agency. Some states issue liquor licenses at the state level, while others issue them at the county or city level. Either way, the state ABC agency must approve the issuance of the liquor licenses. They can send you information to get you on the right path from the beginning. Once you've filed your application for a new

Smart Tip

Make sure your bar is clean and sanitary for your customers. Your public health department will pay particular attention to food-contact surfaces, dishwashing equipment, plumbing, restrooms, sewage disposal, hand-washing facilities, lighting, and ventilation.

You, Under a Microscope

Each state has its own requirements for liquor licenses, but they all have one thing in common: The licensee must be a responsible person. You and your background will be checked thoroughly. They want to make sure you obey the law (you'll have a whole list of laws to abide by as a bar owner) and that you're a financially responsible individual.

To qualify for a liquor license in most states, you must:

- ○ Be at least 21 years of age.
- ○ Be a U.S. citizen.
- ○ Be financially responsible.
- ○ Have a good moral character.

State liquor laws vary, but they generally cover the same topics. Your license will not only determine the type of alcohol you can sell (beer, wine, distilled spirits), but it will also tell you the times and days you can be open for business. Many licenses also regulate renovations, entertainment, advertising, and personnel. Your lawyer can help you fully understand all the liquor laws in your state well before you're ready to open for business.

IRS Form SS-4

Form **SS-4**	**Application for Employer Identification Number**	EIN
(Rev. December 2001) Department of the Treasury Internal Revenue Service	(For use by employers, corporations, partnerships, trusts, estates, churches, government agencies, Indian tribal entities, certain individuals, and others.) ▶ See separate instructions for each line. ▶ Keep a copy for your records.	OMB No. 1545-0003

Type or print clearly.

1 Legal name of entity (or individual) for whom the EIN is being requested

2 Trade name of business (if different from name on line 1)

3 Executor, trustee, "care of" name

4a Mailing address (room, apt., suite no. and street, or P.O. box)

5a Street address (if different) (Do not enter a P.O. box.)

4b City, state, and ZIP code

5b City, state, and ZIP code

6 County and state where principal business is located

7a Name of principal officer, general partner, grantor, owner, or trustor

7b SSN, ITIN, or EIN

8a **Type of entity** (check only one box)
- ☐ Sole proprietor (SSN) _____
- ☐ Partnership
- ☐ Corporation (enter form number to be filed) ▶ _____
- ☐ Personal service corp.
- ☐ Church or church-controlled organization
- ☐ Other nonprofit organization (specify) ▶ _____
- ☐ Other (specify) ▶
- ☐ Estate (SSN of decedent) _____
- ☐ Plan administrator (SSN) _____
- ☐ Trust (SSN of grantor) _____
- ☐ National Guard   ☐ State/local government
- ☐ Farmers' cooperative   ☐ Federal government/military
- ☐ REMIC   ☐ Indian tribal governments/enterprises
- Group Exemption Number (GEN) ▶ _____

8b If a corporation, name the state or foreign country (if applicable) where incorporated | State | Foreign country

9 **Reason for applying** (check only one box)
- ☐ Started new business (specify type) ▶ _____
- ☐ Hired employees (Check the box and see line 12.)
- ☐ Compliance with IRS withholding regulations
- ☐ Other (specify) ▶
- ☐ Banking purpose (specify purpose) ▶ _____
- ☐ Changed type of organization (specify new type) ▶ _____
- ☐ Purchased going business
- ☐ Created a trust (specify type) ▶ _____
- ☐ Created a pension plan (specify type) ▶ _____

10 Date business started or acquired (month, day, year)

11 Closing month of accounting year

12 First date wages or annuities were paid or will be paid (month, day, year). **Note:** *If applicant is a withholding agent, enter date income will first be paid to nonresident alien. (month, day, year)* . . . . ▶

13 Highest number of employees expected in the next 12 months. **Note:** *If the applicant does not expect to have any employees during the period, enter "-0-."* . . . . | Agricultural | Household | Other

14 Check **one** box that best describes the principal activity of your business.
- ☐ Construction   ☐ Rental & leasing   ☐ Transportation & warehousing
- ☐ Real estate   ☐ Manufacturing   ☐ Finance & insurance
- ☐ Health care & social assistance   ☐ Wholesale–agent/broker
- ☐ Accommodation & food service   ☐ Wholesale–other   ☐ Retail
- ☐ Other (specify)

15 Indicate principal line of merchandise sold; specific construction work done; products produced; or services provided.

16a Has the applicant ever applied for an employer identification number for this or any other business? . . . . ☐ Yes   ☐ No
Note: *If "Yes," please complete lines 16b and 16c.*

16b If you checked "Yes" on line 16a, give applicant's legal name and trade name shown on prior application if different from line 1 or 2 above.
Legal name ▶   Trade name ▶

16c Approximate date when, and city and state where, the application was filed. Enter previous employer identification number if known.
Approximate date when filed (mo., day, year) | City and state where filed | Previous EIN

	Complete this section **only** if you want to authorize the named individual to receive the entity's EIN and answer questions about the completion of this form.	
Third Party Designee	Designee's name	Designee's telephone number (include area code) ( )
	Address and ZIP code	Designee's fax number (include area code) ( )

Under penalties of perjury, I declare that I have examined this application, and to the best of my knowledge and belief, it is true, correct, and complete.

Applicant's telephone number (include area code)
(   )

Name and title (type or print clearly) ▶

Signature ▶   Date ▶

Applicant's fax number (include area code)
(   )

For Privacy Act and Paperwork Reduction Act Notice, see separate instructions.   Cat. No. 16055N   Form **SS-4** (Rev. 12-2001)

IRS Form SS-4, continued

Do I Need an EIN?

File Form SS-4 if the applicant entity does not already have an EIN but is required to show an EIN on any return, statement, or other document.[1] **See also the separate instructions for each line on Form SS-4.**

IF the applicant...	AND...	THEN...
Started a new business	Does not currently have (nor expect to have) employees	Complete lines 1, 2, 4a–6, 8a, and 9–16c.
Hired (or will hire) employees, including household employees	Does not already have an EIN	Complete lines 1, 2, 4a–6, 7a–b (if applicable), 8a, 8b (if applicable), and 9–16c.
Opened a bank account	Needs an EIN for banking purposes only	Complete lines 1–5b, 7a–b (if applicable), 8a, 9, and 16a–c.
Changed type of organization	Either the legal character of the organization or its ownership changed (e.g., you incorporate a sole proprietorship or form a partnership)[2]	Complete lines 1–16c (as applicable).
Purchased a going business[3]	Does not already have an EIN	Complete lines 1–16c (as applicable).
Created a trust	The trust is other than a grantor trust or an IRA trust[4]	Complete lines 1–16c (as applicable).
Created a pension plan as a plan administrator[5]	Needs an EIN for reporting purposes	Complete lines 1, 2, 4a–6, 8a, 9, and 16a–c.
Is a foreign person needing an EIN to comply with IRS withholding regulations	Needs an EIN to complete a Form W-8 (other than Form W-8ECI), avoid withholding on portfolio assets, or claim tax treaty benefits[6]	Complete lines 1–5b, 7a–b (SSN or ITIN optional), 8a–9, and 16a–c.
Is administering an estate	Needs an EIN to report estate income on Form 1041	Complete lines 1, 3, 4a–b, 8a, 9, and 16a–c.
Is a withholding agent for taxes on non-wage income paid to an alien (i.e., individual, corporation, or partnership, etc.)	Is an agent, broker, fiduciary, manager, tenant, or spouse who is required to file **Form 1042,** Annual Withholding Tax Return for U.S. Source Income of Foreign Persons	Complete lines 1, 2, 3 (if applicable), 4a–5b, 7a–b (if applicable), 8a, 9, and 16a–c.
Is a state or local agency	Serves as a tax reporting agent for public assistance recipients under Rev. Proc. 80-4, 1980-1 C.B. 581[7]	Complete lines 1, 2, 4a–5b, 8a, 9, and 16a–c.
Is a single-member LLC	Needs an EIN to file **Form 8832,** Classification Election, for filing employment tax returns, **or** for state reporting purposes[8]	Complete lines 1–16c (as applicable).
Is an S corporation	Needs an EIN to file **Form 2553,** Election by a Small Business Corporation[9]	Complete lines 1–16c (as applicable).

[1] For example, a sole proprietorship or self-employed farmer who establishes a qualified retirement plan, or is required to file excise, employment, alcohol, tobacco, or firearms returns, must have an EIN. **A partnership, corporation, REMIC (real estate mortgage investment conduit), nonprofit organization (church, club, etc.), or farmers' cooperative must use an EIN for any tax-related purpose even if the entity does not have employees.**

[2] However, **do not** apply for a new EIN if the existing entity only **(a)** changed its business name, **(b)** elected on Form 8832 to change the way it is taxed (or is covered by the default rules), or **(c)** terminated its partnership status because at least 50% of the total interests in partnership capital and profits were sold or exchanged within a 12-month period. (The EIN of the terminated partnership should continue to be used. See Regulations section 301.6109-1(d)(2)(iii).)

[3] Do not use the EIN of the prior business unless you became the "owner" of a corporation by acquiring its stock.

[4] However, IRA trusts that are required to file **Form 990-T,** Exempt Organization Business Income Tax Return, must have an EIN.

[5] A plan administrator is the person or group of persons specified as the administrator by the instrument under which the plan is operated.

[6] Entities applying to be a Qualified Intermediary (QI) need a QI-EIN even if they already have an EIN. **See Rev. Proc. 2000-12.**

[7] See also *Household employer* on page 4. **(Note:** State or local agencies may need an EIN for other reasons, e.g., hired employees.)

[8] Most LLCs **do not** need to file Form 8832. See **Limited liability company (LLC)** on page 4 for details on completing Form SS-4 for an LLC.

[9] An existing corporation that is electing or revoking S corporation status should use its previously-assigned EIN.

liquor license or for a transfer, you can expect an ABC investigation to take 45 to 60 days, depending on the state. If you're approved, you may have to wait an additional 30 days or longer to actually receive the license. So you can see why you should get started on this process early.

If you've purchased a liquor license from another owner, you may be able to get a temporary permit allowing you to operate the business pending approval of the permanent liquor license. Again, your state's ABC agency can give you all the information on your local requirements and options.

> **⚠ Beware!**
>
> If you owe taxes, it's your responsibility to know it! Severe fines and even imprisonment can be the punishment for not paying your taxes.

Since many liquor licenses are issued based on population, some states aren't issuing any new licenses. If you plan to locate your bar in such a state, you'll have to purchase a license from an existing owner. This means the price of your license depends on what the owner wants for it. You can spend a few thousand dollars to tens of thousands of dollars on your liquor license alone. Before your liquor license will be issued, you must have your food-service license, fire permit, and building permit (if you're doing construction or renovations). So let's get started on those.

Food-Service Licenses

If you plan to serve food in your bar, you'll need a license to do so. The purpose of this license is to make sure you maintain a safe, sanitary environment for your customers. Generally, these licenses are issued for a year and must be renewed. Depending on the size of your bar, the type of equipment you have, and how extensive your menu is, the cost of this license starts at about $35, and goes up from there. The state public health department oversees the licenses and permits, but some allow local or county departments to issue them and conduct inspections.

For you to obtain a food-service license, most states require a floor plan of the layout or proposed layout of your establishment. You must show the placement of all major equipment as well as the location of restrooms and sinks. You'll most likely have to provide a sample menu and a list of the materials you plan to use for cleaning.

A week or two before you open your doors, you should schedule an inspection with the health department to make sure you're in compliance with all applicable laws and regulations. You can also expect to have periodic inspections by the health department throughout the operation of your business.

The Feds

While most of the licenses and permits for your bar are issued on the state or local level, you'll also need to deal with the federal government. For many years, the Bureau of Alcohol, Tobacco and Firearms (ATF) regulated retail bar businesses. The Homeland Security Act of 2002 resulted in the creation of the TTB, which took over regulation duties from the ATF. The TTB used to levy a Special Occupational Tax (SOT), but that has been permanently repealed. While you no longer have to pay the SOT, you do need to complete the SOT registration process with the TTB. You need to register before you begin selling any alcohol, and again if you make any change to your business (such as a change of address or name). If you have any questions regarding the SOT, contact the TTB's National Revenue Center at (800) 937-8864 or visit its website at ttb.gov/nrc.

A Matter of Record

Bar owners must keep detailed records of all liquor, wine, and beer received from suppliers. Your records must include the date and quantity of everything you receive and the name of your supplier. If you don't think you can keep up with a record book, you also have the option of keeping all the invoices and bills for the distilled spirits, wine, and beer you receive. Either way, you must keep some record of this information. If you're inspected by a federal officer and you don't have these records, you may be subject to fines of up to $10,000 and imprisonment for up to five years.

Did Someone Say "Fire"?

The fire department is another agency you want to have a good relationship with. Some state and local laws require a permit from the fire department before you can open your doors. Other areas don't require permits, but the fire department or fire marshal's office conducts periodic inspections to find out if you're following regulations. If you don't meet their standards, you'll receive a citation and have to pay a fine.

It's the fire department that tells you how many patrons you can have in your bar without causing a safety hazard. It bases the number on state and local fire codes and the square footage of your establishment. Although it wants you to be successful and have a full-to-capacity bar, the fire department also has to look out for the well-being of your customers. If a fire or other emergency happened with too many people in the bar, someone could easily get hurt. You don't want that to happen, and neither do the fire marshals. So it's best to work together to ensure the safety of your business.

> **Beware!**
> If you're building your bar or making extensive renovations to an existing building, be sure you have the proper electrical systems, ventilation, and heating and air conditioning equipment to meet your local fire codes. If you're adding space or equipment, check with a licensed electrician to make sure your electrical supply will meet the load the new fixtures demand.

▲

Special Tax Registration Form

OMB NO. 1513-0112 (11/30/2005)

DEPARTMENT OF THE TREASURY
ALCOHOL AND TOBACCO TAX AND TRADE BUREAU
SPECIAL TAX REGISTRATION AND RETURN
ALCOHOL AND TOBACCO
(Please Read Instructions Carefully Before Completing This Form)

SECTION I - TAXPAYER IDENTIFYING INFORMATION

1. EMPLOYER IDENTIFICATION NUMBER *(Required see instructions)*	2. BUSINESS TELEPHONE NUMBER ( )	FOR TTB USE ONLY
3. NAME *(Last, First, Middle)* or	CORPORATE NAME *(If Corporation)*	T
4. TRADE NAME		FF
		FP
5. MAILING ADDRESS *(Street address or P.O. box number)*		I
6. CITY STATE ZIP CODE		T

ACTUAL LOCATION *(IF DIFFERENT THAN ABOVE)*
7. PHYSICAL ADDRESS OF PRINCIPAL PLACE OF BUSINESS *(Show street address)*

8. CITY   STATE   ZIP CODE

9. TAX PERIOD COVERING
(only one tax period per form)

FROM: _____
(mm/dd/yyyy)

TO: June 30, _____
(yyyy)

SECTION II - TAX COMPUTATION

TAX CLASS DESCRIPTION (FOR ITEMS MARKED*, SEE INSTRUCTIONS) (a)		MONTHLY (b)	ANNUAL (c)	LOCATIONS (d)	TAX DUE (e)	CODE (f)
RETAIL DEALER	Liquors *(Distilled spirits, wine or beer)*	$20.83 $^1/_3$	$250			11
	Beer only	$20.83 $^1/_3$	250			12
	Liquors (Distilled Spirits, Wine or Beer) - at large	$20.83 $^1/_3$	250			15
	Beer only - at large	$20.83 $^1/_3$	250			16
WHOLESALE DEALER	Distilled spirits, wine or beer	$41.66 $^2/_3$	500			31
	Beer only	$41.66 $^2/_3$	500			32
BREWER	Regular rate	$83.33 $^1/_3$	1000			41
	REDUCED rate*	$41.66 $^2/_3$	500			43*
NONBEVERAGE DRAWBACK CLAIMANT			500			51
INDUSTRIAL ALCOHOL	User of specially denatured alcohol	$20.83 $^1/_3$	250			55
	Dealer in specially denatured alcohol	$20.83 $^1/_3$	250			56
	User of tax-free alcohol	$20.83 $^1/_3$	250			57
ALCOHOL PRODUCERS	Proprietor of alcohol fuel plant	$83.33 $^1/_3$	1000			58
	Proprietor of alcohol fuel plant - REDUCED*	$41.66 $^2/_3$	500			59*
	Proprietor of distilled spirits plant	$83.33 $^1/_3$	1000			81
	Proprietor of distilled spirits plant - REDUCED*	$41.66 $^2/_3$	500			86*
	Proprietor of bonded wine cellar	$83.33 $^1/_3$	1000			82
	Proprietor of bonded wine cellar - REDUCED*	$41.66 $^2/_3$	500			87*
	Proprietor of bonded wine warehouse	$83.33 $^1/_3$	1000			83
	Proprietor of bonded wine warehouse - REDUCED*	$41.66 $^2/_3$	500			88*
	Proprietor of taxpaid wine bottling house	$83.33 $^1/_3$	1000			84
	Proprietor of taxpaid wine bottling house - REDUCED*	$41.66 $^2/_3$	500			89*
TOBACCO PRODUCTS	Manufacturer of tobacco products	$83.33 $^1/_3$	1000			91
	Manufacturer of tobacco products - REDUCED*	$41.66 $^2/_3$	500			95*
	Manufacturer of cigarette papers and tubes	$83.33 $^1/_3$	1000			92
	Manufacturer of cigarette papers and tubes - REDUCED*	$41.66 $^2/_3$	500			96*
	Proprietor of export warehouse	$83.33 $^1/_3$	1000			93
	Proprietor of export warehouse - REDUCED*	$41.66 $^2/_3$	500			97*

MAKE CHECK OR MONEY ORDER PAYABLE TO "ALCOHOL AND TOBACCO TAX AND TRADE BUREAU", **WRITE YOUR EMPLOYER IDENTIFICATION NUMBER ON THE CHECK AND SEND IT WITH THE RETURN TO TTB, P.O. BOX 371962, PITTSBURGH, PA 15250-7962.**   TOTAL TAX DUE $

Under penalties of perjury, I declare that the statements in this return/registration are true and correct to the best of my knowledge and belief; that this return/registration applies only to the specified business and location or, where the return/registration is for more than one location, it applies only to the businesses at the locations specified on the attached list. Note: Violation of Title 26, United States Code 7206, with the respect to a declaration under the penalties of perjury, is punishable upon conviction by a fine of not more than $100,000 *($500,000 in the case of a corporation)* or imprisonment for not more than 3 years, or both, with the costs of prosecution added thereto.

SIGNATURE	TITLE	DATE

TTB F 5630.5 (5/2005)

Special Tax Registration Form, continued

SECTION III - BUSINESS REGISTRATION

10. OWNERSHIP INFORMATION: *(Check One Box Only)* ☐ INDIVIDUAL OWNER ☐ PARTNERSHIP ☐ CORPORATION ☐ LLC ☐ OTHER *(Specify)* _____

11. OWNERSHIP RESPONSIBILITY: (Read instruction sheet; use a separate sheet of paper if additional space is needed.)

FULL NAME	ADDRESS	POSITION
FULL NAME	ADDRESS	POSITION
FULL NAME	ADDRESS	POSITION
FULL NAME	ADDRESS	POSITION
FULL NAME	ADDRESS	POSITION

12. ☐ GROSS RECEIPTS less than $500,000 *(See instructions for reduced rate taxpayers on the attached instruction sheet)*

13. ☐ NEW BUSINESS *(NOTE: RETAILERS AND WHOLESALERS SHOW DATE ALCOHOLIC BEVERAGE SALES BEGAN; PRODUCERS, MANUFACTURERS AND USERS SHOW DATE BUSINESS COMMENCED)* | DATE OF CHANGE (mm, dd, yyyy)

14. ☐ EXISTING BUSINESS WITH CHANGE IN:

	DATE OF CHANGE
☐ (a) NAME/TRADE NAME *(Indicate)*	DATE OF CHANGE *(mm, dd, yyyy)*
☐ (b) ADDRESS *(Indicate)*	DATE OF CHANGE *(mm, dd, yy)yy*
☐ (c) OWNERSHIP *(Indicate)*	DATE OF CHANGE *(mm, dd, yyyy)*
☐ (d) EMPLOYER IDENTIFICATION NUMBER (OLD: NEW:)	DATE OF CHANGE *(mm, dd, yyyy)*
☐ (e) BUSINESS TELEPHONE NUMBER ( )	

15. ☐ DISCONTINUED BUSINESS | DATE BUSINESS DISCONTINUED *(mm, dd, yyyy)*

PAPERWORK REDUCTION ACT NOTICE

This request is in accordance with the Paperwork Reduction Act of 1995. This information is used to ensure compliance by taxpayers of P.L. 100-647, Technical Corrections Act of 1988, and the Internal Revenue Laws of the United States. The information collection is used to determine and collect the right amount of tax.

The estimated average burden associated with this collection of information is .8 hours per respondent or recordkeeper, depending on individual circumstances. Comments concerning the accuracy of this burden estimate and suggestions for reducing this burden should be addressed to Reports Management Officer, Regulations and Procedures Division, Alcohol and Tobacco Tax and Trade Bureau, Washington, D.C. 20220.

An agency may not conduct or sponsor, and a person is not required to respond to, a collection of information unless it displays a currently valid OMB control number.

(SEE INSTRUCTION SHEET)

TTB F 5630.5 (5/2005)

▲

Some of the other things the fire department will verify are:

- *Fire extinguishers.* You need to have a certain type and number of these, based on the size of your bar, with proper placement.
- *Exits.* You must have an adequate number of exits in your bar that aren't obstructed by equipment or furnishings. They must also have lighted exit signs above the doors.
- *Smoke detectors and fire suppression devices.* You must have smoke detectors to warn of a fire. Some states also require other equipment to put out the fire, such as sprinklers or dry chemical dispensers. If you have a sprinkler system, you're not allowed to block or cover it in any way.

Miscellaneous Permits

Depending on what kind of bar you'll have, where it's located, and whether or not you're doing any construction, you may have a whole battery of other permits to contend with. Get together with your lawyer to find out all the permits you'll need for your individual situation. Here are a few of the permits you might need:

- *Sign permit.* Some communities have a specific agency that regulates signage. Many of these agencies require a sign permit. Other areas have restrictions on size, lighting, and placement. Of course, your landlord may have policies regarding signage, too.
- *Building permit.* If you're building a bar from the ground up, you should check with your local zoning board and city planning board before you put any money into it. Any kind of remodeling or construction generally requires a certain type of building permit.
- *Seller's permit.* If you'll be collecting sales tax on any goods or services you sell, you may be required to obtain a permit. Check with your state and local authorities.
- *Health permit.* Some locations require you to have a permit from the Board of Health if you're selling any food or beverages.
- *Historical commission permit.* If your location is in a designated historical building, you may not be able to make certain renovations. Check with the historical commission before you start drawing up extravagant plans!

Protecting Yourself and Your Bar

As a bar owner, you have certain obligations and responsibilities to your customers, employees, and community. If you don't take that responsibility seriously, you could end up losing your bar and your personal standing in the community.

From intoxicated guests to sexually harassed employees, you need to know what's happening in your place of business. If you rely on general managers to take care of these details, be sure they have the training they need in these areas. They can then train all of your employees to prevent your exposure to these liabilities. Remember: It's ultimately your responsibility and your business that's at risk.

Although most of these issues won't come into play until your bar is open, it's crucial that you're aware of them right upfront. You may find out how much is at risk and

Walking a Straight Line

Although you can't eliminate your liability risk due to intoxicated customers, you can put a number of practices in place to reduce the potential. Here are six ideas you can implement to catch the problem before it gets out of hand.

1. *Make sure all your employees are fully trained on alcohol awareness.* Most communities have training programs in place to ensure local bars are educated in this area. You may also want to conduct periodic in-house refresher courses.

2. *Create a booklet of policies and procedures for your managers, bartenders, and servers.* Give it to new employees when they're hired. This can eliminate the question of who to turn to when a delicate situation arises.

3. *Keep an incident log behind the bar.* Your bartenders and servers can enter the date, time, and occurrence when they have to refuse service to a customer. This can help your case if you're ever in a legal situation.

4. *Offer free snacks, such as peanuts or popcorn, to slow down your guests' consumption rate.* While eating salty snacks may seem to encourage customers to drink more, customers who indulge in these snacks actually drink at a slower rate, and that's more important than how much they drink. If you offer happy hour, which encourages customers to drink within a specified time, it's a good idea to provide free appetizers to prevent excessive drinking.

5. *Provide free coffee to all customers.* You might also consider offering free sodas or other nonalcoholic drinks for designated drivers.

6. *Keep the names and phone numbers of taxi companies near each phone.* Encourage your bartenders and servers to offer to call a cab for customers who may have had too much to drink. Or if the employees are too busy, have them ask a manager to do it.

decide the bar business isn't for you. It's better to find out early—before you have put a ton of money into it.

Alcohol Awareness

Monitoring intoxication and alcohol abuse is your number-one priority as a bar owner—at all times. Whether it involves your customers or your employees, you need to be aware of alcohol and how it's affecting your business. It's a powerful product, and you need to make sure your employees dispense it properly. Drunk driving is still a major concern in the United States, and bars are a prime target for liability.

Some states require all bartenders, managers, and servers to have a permit to serve alcohol. This permit involves alcohol awareness training and a commitment to ensure the safety of the community when it comes to drunk driving. You should also consider obtaining liquor liability insurance or third-party liability insurance to protect your business from lawsuits

> **Bright Idea**
> Keep an *ID Checking Guide* from the Drivers License Guide Co. at the door or behind the bar. These books include pictures of state and international identification cards along with information to help you catch fake IDs. To order a guide, call (800) 227-8827 or go to driverslicenseguide.com.

related to intoxicated customers who cause damage to other people or property. You may not be able to eliminate your liability when it comes to intoxication, but you can take many steps to reduce the risk involved.

You can establish your bar as an ethical establishment from day one by putting several tools into effect to prevent customers from drinking too much and potentially causing damage in the community. If a liability situation comes up, you can also use all the safeguards you've set up as part of your defense.

Sexual Harassment

All businesses must contend with the possibility of sexual harassment. Bars and restaurants are absolutely no exception. Every year, millions of dollars are awarded to complainants in sexual harassment cases in the United States, so you can see how this is a serious issue for employers.

According to Ira Michael Shepard, a labor and employment law attorney with Saul Ewing, LLP in Washington, DC, statistics show that a sexual harassment lawsuit is one of the biggest threats to employers today. "Make sure that your reason [for termination] isn't related at all to anything that could be considered sexual harassment," says Shepard. "For example, if a supervisor is terminating a waitress because she won't go out with him, that's illegal. Avoid even the appearance of harassment."

The Equal Employment Opportunity Commission (EEOC) has issued standards to determine the liability of an employer for acts of sexual harassment. The guidelines encourage business owners to have an effective anti-harassment policy and complaint procedure. You can include your policies in your employee handbook, which you can give to your staff when they're hired. Here are some tips for composing your bar's sexual harassment policy:

 Beware!

Don't limit sexual harassment education to your managers. The harasser can be the victim's supervisor, a supplier, a supervisor of another area, a co-worker, or a nonemployee. Sexual harassment can often interfere with an individual's work performance, and it may create an intimidating, hostile, or offensive work environment for your staff.

- Give the staff a clear explanation of what actions are considered harassment.
- Make sure your employees understand that they won't be subject to any kind of retaliation if they make complaints or provide information.
- Design a standard complaint process. (Don't make it too difficult or complex.)
- Treat complaints confidentially.
- Include a quick, thorough, and impartial investigation in the procedure.
- If the investigation shows that harassment has occurred, assure employees that immediate and appropriate corrective action will be taken.

For a complete overview of sexual harassment standards and other discrimination laws, you can go to the EEOC's website at eeoc.gov.

How to Get Your Favorite Paper: Money!

Now that we've reached the summit on the mountain of paperwork involved in the bar business, let's get to the good part—financing. You may be thinking to yourself "Financing isn't the good part; it's a nightmare!" Sure, it involves a whole lot of paperwork, too. But when all is said and done, it's our favorite kind of paper that comes out of it in the end, right?

If you don't already have the money to finance your bar, you have a number of options. According to bar management consultant Bob Johnson of Clearwater, South Carolina, getting an unsecured loan is very unlikely in the bar business. "There have to be some assets," says Johnson. "I think most of the startup money comes from disposable income. There are a lot of professionals who form partnerships among themselves or people who have made money in the stock market, and they invest in things like bars and hotels—it's very common."

If you don't already have your startup capital, you can try to enlist a group of partners. Or you can try to get a bank loan. To find a list of lenders, you should contact your local Small Business Development Center, which is part of the SBA. They're not affiliated with any particular lenders, but they can provide a list of lenders who work with startup bars and nightclubs.

> ## Smart Tip
> Tip...
>
> If you're going to present your business plan to a bank for a loan, be sure to include a minimum of two years on your projected income—profit, loss, and cash flow. The more solid business information you provide, the better your chances of getting approved.

Getting a bank loan is difficult, but not impossible, says Maggie Mui, a senior vice president with Wells Fargo. "You need a great business plan that clearly explains what you're trying to do, your target market, and your competition," she says. "It also helps if you can demonstrate that you've found a niche market to target."

Your business plan must include detailed financials, such as the predicted income vs. expenses of the bar you'll run, she says. You also must demonstrate that you have experience and background in the industry; most banks won't approve loans for people without it. It also helps if you're taking over an established business that has a proven track record, she says.

Mui says the bank looks at several factors when considering business loans. Those factors can be summarized as what she calls the "five C's": Character, Condition, Capital, Capacity, and Collateral. Here's an overview of each:

- *Character.* This is the overall impression you give the lender, Mui says. It's not just looking and acting professional; it also relates to your credit history. The bank will look at your personal credit history and your FICO score. If you have tax liens, the bank will know about it—and so should you. Before you apply for a loan, make sure you carefully examine your credit report and resolve any errors or outstanding issues.
- *Condition.* This refers to how—exactly—you plan to use the money you're seeking. Do you need it to buy equipment? Or do you need a line of credit? There are many different types of loans, and what you plan to use the money for will allow the bank to determine if any of them are a good fit for you. If you have a good business plan, you'll know exactly what you need the money for, Mui says.
- *Capital.* The bank will want to know how much of your own money is invested in your business. You can't expect a bank to finance 100 percent of your business,

Mui says. If you haven't invested a dime of your own money, it's not going to work she says. "This is how we know you're committed to your business," Mui says.

- *Capacity*. You'll need to show the bank how you're going to pay back the loan. This means providing a detailed breakdown of your cash flow and monthly income, Mui says. This helps the bank approve the loan and determine the terms, including the length of the loan and the monthly payment. You'll also need to show that you have alternative means to pay back the loan if your business faces unexpected challenges. For example, Mui says, you'll want to show the bank that if you get sick, your partner will be able to keep things running until you're able to return to work.

- *Collateral*. Any form of collateral will allow your loan to be considered a secured loan, which means you're likely to get a lower interest rate. Your collateral may be your building—if you're buying one—or any of the equipment you have. "If it's not fixed to the walls and has a depreciation value, then it can be collateral," Mui says.

A sixth "C" that banks may consider is customer, Mui says. It may help your chances of securing a loan if you're an existing customer at that bank: It's a good way for the bank to know and trust you more.

Mui says a banker can help you with your finances even if you aren't seeking a loan. "It's a tough time to be a small business owner right now. People are spending less, so business owners have to be more creative to attract customers," she says. "Business owners need to clean up their finances. Go see a banker, and have a financial review. They can help you find ways to save money, and make more money."

Spending That Pile of Cash

The bar/club industry can be a pricey undertaking. Because of the high failure rate, you may come across desperate bar owners who are willing to take a low purchase price just to get out of the business. You'll also find that startup costs for bars vary depending on their size, location, and target market. So we can't give you a concrete amount for what you can expect to pay to start your business.

We spoke with one entrepreneur in California who spent $25,000 taking over someone else's bar. Another bar owner in Florida spent several million dollars starting his club (and he didn't even build the building). The numbers vary all across the board. Your bar's size, location, type, and concept will make your startup costs as individual as your business.

However, the "Startup Expenses" on page 61 will give you some idea of what you'll be looking at—from the low end to the high end. Again, you could buy an existing bar that would nullify all the numbers on our low-end chart or start a large-scale club that's off the map from our high-end numbers. You'll have to do some research to find out what your bar will cost based on your concept, size, and location. Once you have your research in hand, you can use the "Startup Expenses Worksheet" on page 62 to tally up your own expenses.

Now that we have all the paperwork out of the way—licenses, permits, laws, and money—we'll start looking at how to design the layout of your bar and how to decorate it. In the next chapter, we'll pull out our pencils and start mapping out where everything should go and how it should look to match your bar's concept and clientele.

Startup Expenses

Here are the startup costs for two hypothetical bars. The first, Night Owl, is a tavern with a maximum capacity of 100 people and serves only beer and wine with a limited menu. Night Owl has annual sales of $327,416. The second, Neverland, is a 1,000-person-capacity nightclub with a full-service bar. Located in the downtown area of a metropolitan city, Neverland has annual sales of $976,132.

Expenses	Night Owl	Neverland
Rent (security deposit and first month)	$4,000	$7,500
Leasehold improvements (heating/air conditioning, electrical, plumbing, painting, carpentry, sign, flooring, smoke detectors)	$18,000	$65,000
Equipment/fixtures	$40,000	$225,000
Licenses/permits	$5,000	$20,000
Beginning inventory	$22,000	$38,000
Phone/utilities deposits	$150	$375
Payroll	$5,550	$18,730
Grand opening marketing	$1,000	$3,000
Legal services	$1,000	$3,000
Accounting	$250	$650
Insurance	$500	$3,000
Miscellaneous expenses (add roughly 10% of total)	$9,745	$38,425
Total Startup Costs	**$107,195**	**$422,680**

▲

Startup Expenses Worksheet

Expenses

Rent (security deposit and first month) $_____

Leasehold improvements   _____
(heating/air conditioning, electrical,
plumbing, painting, carpentry, sign,
flooring, smoke detectors)

Equipment/fixtures   _____

Licenses/permits   _____

Beginning inventory   _____

Phone/utilities deposits   _____

Payroll   _____

Grand opening marketing   _____

Legal services   _____

Accounting   _____

Insurance   _____

Miscellaneous expenses   _____
(add roughly 10% of total)

Total Startup Costs $_____

Everything In Its Place:
Bar Layout

Once you have all your paperwork filled out and filed, and you've lined up your financing, you can start designing your dream and deciding how you're going to spend your money. In this chapter, we'll take you step by step through creating your layout and shaping your food and drink menu. If you decided to purchase an existing bar, this part may simply involve some remodeling. Or you may decide to keep a good portion of the established equipment but completely change the atmosphere and décor. It's in this phase of the process of opening your own bar that you can begin to see the theme you've chosen come to life.

But first things first: You need to measure each room to see exactly how much space you have. If you have room in your budget and you have a large facility, you might consider hiring an architect or interior designer to help you design your bar's unique personality. Ron Newman, the sports bar owner in Manhattan Beach, California, says that, initially, he couldn't afford this type of help, but now he's able to use both a kitchen designer and an interior designer at his venues. "If you see something you like, take a picture of it," he suggests. Then you can work with your designer—or even by yourself—to replicate that look in your own bar. Keep your budget in mind, though—you don't want to go overboard before you even get started!

When you came up with your name, theme, and concept, you may have already decided some of the ways they would fit into your design. You want to continue that vision in every aspect of your bar. As soon as the customer walks in the door, every little detail contributes to the overall atmosphere. You want your clientele to keep coming back because they like the feel of the place, as well as for all the other great things you offer. Your bar's atmosphere will also be part of how your customers will describe it to their friends.

Smart Tip

Before you get started on the layout and design of your bar, write down your concept, how it will appeal to your clientele, and how you envision the atmosphere and décor. Keep this with you whenever you're making design decisions or looking at options so you stay on track with your concept from start to finish.

From the Outside In

Your concept actually starts on the street. Your signage should not only draw attention to your bar but also follow the theme your customers see on the inside. If your exterior has a clean, simple design, you might keep that consistent on the inside, too. If you have an old-time rustic exterior, you can continue that inside with your barstools and glassware. If you have the financial ability, you might think about remodeling your exterior to match your theme, and make it as inviting as possible.

When it comes to your interior design, your first goal should be to maintain your concept and theme without sacrificing service efficiency. Next, you want to keep in mind the ambience—you want to make your clientele feel comfortable so they can come in, relax, and have a good time.

Lights, Camera, Action!

One way to set the mood in your bar is through your choice of lighting. You can choose bright lights and lots of windows to give a daylight effect. If your location provides a beautiful view of a mountain or the ocean, you might want to take advantage of it in your bar. For a club, you may choose a different kind of

> **Beware!**
>
> If you decide to use bright lights or make use of a significant amount of daylight in your bar, keep in mind that these can make dirty areas quite visible.

bright light: neon and dance lights that contrast with darkness. Or you can choose to have a dark, romantic bar with very little lighting at all. The amount of light and the colors you choose can go a long way in establishing the ambience of your bar.

Here are some tips on using lighting to your advantage:

- *If your bar is open during the day, make use of the daylight.* You can install skylights to light up the reception area or to light up plants and indoor trees. Windows, glass doors, and glass walls can also brighten up areas of your bar during the day. You can maximize this free lighting from the sun with mirrors on some walls.

- *Use dimmers on all your lights to create varied effects.* With dimmers, you can make your bar bright during the day and darker after the sun goes down. At the end of the night, you can turn up the lights to let everyone know you're closing. If you change your décor on a regular basis to match different themes, dimmers can make it easier to match the lighting to your décor.

- *Aim the majority of a room's lights on the area you want to be your focal point, whether it's your bar, dance floor, or entertainment area.* Use indirect lighting for less important areas, such as seating. However, you don't want to make it too dark— your customers need to be able to see where they're going!

- *Use lower-cost fixtures in areas like the office, storage area, kitchen, restrooms, and other areas that don't contribute to the atmosphere of your bar.*

All the Colors of the Rainbow

Before you get too involved in the design process, you should make some basic decisions about the overall look of your bar. If you have a large bar, you may choose to have different designs in each room that all follow your main concept. Two important things to think about are your colors and your general environment.

From white to black, the color scheme of your bar will help set the tone. Since colors can go out of fashion over time, you should stay away from trendy color combinations unless you plan to remodel in a few years. One exception to this would be a sports bar decorated with the colors of the local basketball team. Psychological studies show that colors can greatly affect people's moods. Blue makes people feel calm, while red is stimulating and energetic. Colors can also play a part in how intimate or expansive your bar looks. Darker colors make a room seem smaller, while bright colors make it seem larger.

Beware!
If you expect to have loud bands or music playing in your bar, you'll want to look into sound-proofing. Your customers will enjoy the music, but your neighbors may not.

When you're choosing your color scheme, it's important to look at the colors you like under the lighting you have chosen. One color can create a completely different atmosphere under various lighting conditions, and you want to make informed decisions.

Some bars, clubs especially, will change their décor every night to match the theme of the entertainment or crowd coming in on a particular night of the week. For example, the bar may play a different kind of music each night—attracting a different clientele—and match the décor, color, and atmosphere to the style of music. If you have dance and hip-hop music on one night and country music on another night, you probably won't want to use the same décor for both.

Sound Check

Sound will play a large role in your bar's atmosphere, and the fixtures you choose can help control background noise to create the effect you want. Of course, you'll probably have some form of entertainment contributing to the sound, but your décor can add to the background noise. If you want your bar to be loud and boisterous, you should choose fixtures with hard surfaces that will bounce the sound all around the room. If you want a quieter, more intimate atmosphere, you can use textures, such as carpeting, cork, fabrics, and acoustical tiles. All these choices should follow your theme.

Deciding What Goes Where

The layout of your bar depends on the type of bar you'll have, the size and design of your space, and your concept. The first thing to consider when planning your layout is what you want your customers to focus on. Do you want them to be driven to the bar? Or would you rather have them make a beeline for the dance floor? If you have a sports bar, you might want to make a big, flat-screen TV—or several of them—the focal point.

Once you've identified the focal point, you can figure out how to draw attention to it. You can use lighting, seating level, placement, ceiling height, or size relation—

or maybe even all of the above! For example, if you want the dance floor to grab your customers' attention, you might place it in the center of the room, light it up with flashing colored lights, give it the most space in the bar, and have steps leading down to it from small tables surrounding it.

20 Questions

Believe it or not, the design and layout of your bar can make or break your business. Before the moving trucks pull in, ask yourself these 20 questions:

1. Will your bar need to be stocked often?
2. Where will your bartender get supplies?
3. Will employees be able to get to storage and ice machines quickly?
4. Can guests identify your concept at the door?
5. Will anything impede traffic flow to the exits or the bar?
6. Do you have spacious aisles and walkways for your servers?
7. Are your tables able to accommodate groups of various sizes?
8. Are your restroom facilities located in a well-marked, easy-to-find area?
9. Are pay phones in a quiet area?
10. Do bartenders have easy access to a telephone to call taxis for customers?
11. If your bar serves food, is there an intercom system between the bar and kitchen?
12. Are fire exits and safety equipment easily accessible?
13. Is your service station at the bar easily accessible to servers without impeding customer traffic?
14. If you're in a cold climate, do you have a coat-check area or space to hang coats?
15. Based on your layout plans, how easy will it be to clean your bar?
16. Does your color scheme match the concept of your bar?
17. Do your employees have easy access to a restroom?
18. Is your bar visible upon entry to the establishment?
19. Is there enough space for your bartenders to get around behind the bar?
20. Does your layout have the ability to expand when your business becomes wildly successful?

> **Beware!**
>
> When deciding on the layout of your bar, don't forget to include plenty of back-office and storage space. You'll need an area where you can handle shipping and receiving, do your bookkeeping and other paperwork, and store inventory for those busy weekend nights!

Many bar owners want the bar to be the focus. After all, you want your customers to buy drinks, right? The bar can run the entire length of the room opposite the entrance, or it can be an island bar in the center of the room with seating around it. If you have plenty of space, you might consider using the bar to separate the entertainment areas. It could act as the dividing line between the dance floor or stage and a quieter lounge area where people can talk more easily. You can also have one main bar with smaller bars that can be used when the place gets hopping.

While you design around your focal point, you need to be realistic. Keep in mind the flow of traffic and provide plenty of space and mobility for your bartenders and servers. You can use your layout to restrict or enhance the traffic flow. Unless all your customers receive their drinks from servers, you want the bar to be noticeable and easy to reach. You don't want to make it difficult for people to get to the bar for their drinks. Make a clear path, not an obstacle course. If you have servers, place their stations at the bar in an easily accessible location, too, with a quick, easy path to their tables. If you have a kitchen, keep your servers and bartenders in mind when deciding its location, too. You don't want your layout to restrict your employees' ability to deliver quick, efficient service.

Check out the sample bar layouts on the next page. You may decide not to use one of these designs, but they can give you a starting point for designing your own bar.

Finding a Place to Sit

Determining your seating layout is one of the most important parts of designing your bar layout. Smaller neighborhood bars generally have an open floor plan with tables for group seating. On the other hand, clubs try to encourage patrons to dance or circulate, so they don't want all their customers sitting at tables. When purchasing tables and chairs, ask yourself "How comfortable do I want my customers to be?"

> **Beware!**
>
> When purchasing chairs for your bar, don't buy wooden chairs that have spokes on the backrest. They tend to break easily and will need to be replaced frequently.

You can choose from various heights of tables and chairs, too. For instance, at a club, you might want 42-inch-tall tables and bar stools. This way, if a person is standing next to someone seated, they will still be at about the

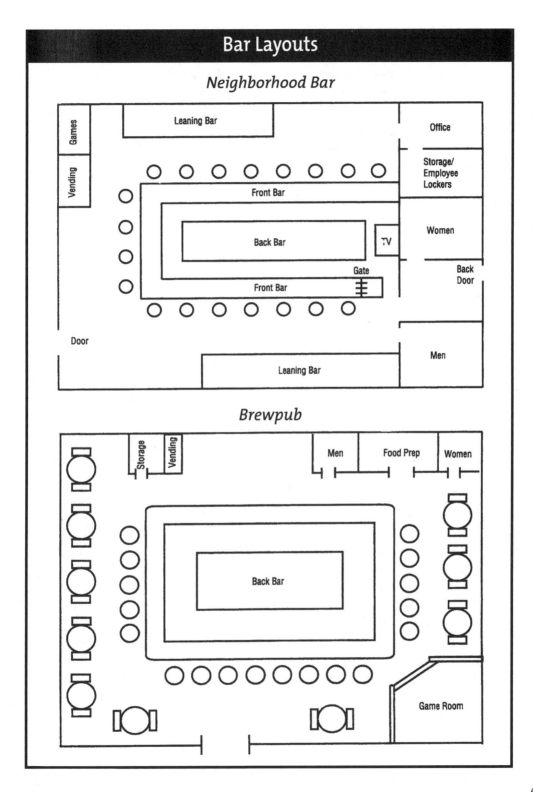

same eye level. Tables in a lounge might measure 30 inches high.

If you have the space, you might consider putting one or two VIP rooms or booths in your bar. These provide another way to generate income for your business. Customers can pay a fee in advance to reserve the area for private parties of two to 20 people. What's a VIP? "A VIP in South Beach is anybody who makes a reservation to come and sit in a VIP room,

> **Beware!**
> As you start planning your food and drink menu, brainstorm some appetizers, entrees, and special drink recipes that could match your theme. Write them all down!

which is normally a two-bottle minimum—bottles being approximately $250 each," says Gerry Kelly, the Miami club manager.

Most VIP rooms have their own staff that's trained to give top-notch service. "We have VIP runners who escort VIPs from the front door to their table," Kelly explains. "The runners will seat them at the table and then bring a VIP server over to wait on them. We also have a VIP director who's responsible for the booking and service for all VIPs who reserve tables. He also schedules the VIP staff based on the size of the events and the number of VIP reservations." If you don't have the space to provide an entire room, you can create private VIP booths by separating them with curtains. If you do have the space, you can go all out with your VIP rooms. Kelly says at The Fifth, they have private VIP suites, some with their own elevators and entrances. The suites can be rented out for $5,000 a night, plus a four- or five-bottle minimum.

Flexible Layout

Your bar or nightclub may be packed on the weekends, but you may find yourself with room to spare during the week. One way to generate additional business during these slower times is to make your venue available for private events. Kelly says his club, The Fifth, generates 60 percent of its revenue by hosting corporate events during the week. Companies pay a room rental fee, and pre-purchase the liquor for the event. The rooms are set up according to the type of event; Kelly's club will do a full sit-down dinner or cocktail parties.

Keep this potential source of revenue in mind when designing your bar or club. Try to design a layout that will allow you to accommodate private parties—big or small. And then go out and market yourself to companies or families who may be looking for a place to hold their next get-together.

Menu Planning 101

In the next chapter, we'll begin discussing the kind of equipment you'll need for your bar. But before we go that far, you'll need to have a pretty good idea of what you're going to serve. Are you going to have a full bar or just serve beer and wine? Are you going to serve food? Are you going to serve appetizers and sandwiches or offer full lunch and dinner menus? Make sure you have a clear idea of all the equipment you'll need to provide these services before you start buying stuff. You don't want to go over your budget just because you didn't plan.

If you'll be serving full meals, you don't have to map out the entire menu right away. This is something you can discuss with your chef once you're closer to opening. Just keep in mind the type of food you'll be offering and what kind of staff and equipment you'll need to prepare it. If you just want to serve snacks, like popcorn and peanuts, keep in mind that these types of food can be messy. For small snacks, you'll need to assign someone to complete regularly scheduled cleanings throughout the night. Otherwise, your bar will look like a disaster area!

Make a sample menu with feature items you would like to serve. If you're going to serve sandwiches, write down whether you want to offer both cold and hot sandwiches. If you're going to have just an appetizer selection, write down what kind of appetizers you would like to have. Keep your concept in mind when making food choices. If you have a Mexican fiesta-themed bar, you don't want to have a menu filled with Chinese food, right?

Once you have your layout mapped out and a rough idea of your type of menu, move on to Chapter 7, where we'll go over the kind of equipment you'll need to make all this happen. In Chapter 8, we'll discuss suppliers, liquor selection, and inventory, so pull out that clipboard and let's make a shopping list!

If You Equip It, They Will Come:
Equipment

Your design is done. Your basic menu is planned. You've secured financing. Now it's time to think about spending some money on equipment. In this chapter, we'll help you figure out what equipment you'll need to get your bar up and running. From fixtures to glassware to back-office equipment, like computers and telephones, you'll need to have it all.

This is the expensive part of starting a bar, but we'll give you some options to help control your costs.

The important thing to keep in mind when you're equipping your bar is what will really matter to the profitability of your business. Will spending $500 per imported Scandanavian chair make your customers any happier than $100 bar stools built in the United States? These are decisions you'll have to make throughout the buying process. You'll want to analyze each purchase carefully. For each piece of equipment, ask yourself if the equipment will do the job efficiently, match your décor, fit into your available space, and enhance your overall profitability. Then you'll need to assess whether the cost is reasonable for the purpose it will serve and how it compares to other estimates you've gotten.

Knowing your target clientele is essential when furnishing and equipping your establishment. Do they know the difference between ritzy and cost-conscious? Do they care? How sophisticated do you think they are, and why do you think that? Remember, bar owners don't succeed simply by pouring money into their operation. Examples of "hole in the wall" bars that rake in piles of money can be found all over the United States. Likewise, many cases exist where millions have been spent on the preparation of a drinking establishment resulting only in empty rooms.

How much money you spend on your equipment will depend on your product, whether you serve food, and what kind of entertainment you want to provide. By the time you're ready to purchase your equipment, you'll have a clear concept, location, and name, and you'll have figured out your market and defined your clientele. Many of your equipment decisions will be based on all the other work and planning you've done so far.

Buying New or Used?

When you're equipping your bar, you have a number of options when it comes to making the actual purchases. You can buy new equipment, you can buy used equipment, or you can lease equipment. Bob Brenlin, the neighborhood pub owner in Seattle, bought the equipment for his bar, Fiddler's Inn, but when he needed to renovate another of his Seattle pubs, Latona, he leased equipment. "It's not a bad idea if you can stamp out the right lease, but you can also depreciate equipment you own. So upgrading to a lease is kind of a trade-off. You have to talk to your accountant to figure out which one's the best." Ron Newman, a sports bar owner in Manhattan Beach, California, acquired his equipment in a variety of ways. "Initially, we got most of our bar equipment at auctions," says Newman. "Our sound equipment and stuff like that we bought new. Our furniture and kitchen equipment was bought used."

Bright Idea

Many equipment vendors are happy to help you choose the right type of equipment for your particular bar. You can benefit from their experience by asking them about other bars they've worked with that may be similar to yours. These vendors know all about the latest products; plus, they can help you stay within your budget.

Because many bars and restaurants go out of business, you might find great deals on equipment at local and regional auctions. You'll even find advertisements for used equipment in the newspaper or online, at sites like Craigslist. If you end up buying used equipment, be sure to inspect it carefully. Check for cracks, especially around the welding and joint areas. If you have the time, find out if replacement parts are still available for that particular piece of equipment.

You can save a great deal of money on startup costs by leasing equipment. Generally, leases will last between 24 and 48 months, and many companies offer an option to buy at the end of the lease for a fraction of the original cost. Most bar owners lease some equipment, such as ice machines. You can work with the supplier to get extra perks like a 24-hour service agreement. Some suppliers will even offer free service and repair or replace equipment at no charge. Keep in mind, though, that if your bar goes out of business, you may be stuck paying for equipment you're no longer using.

The Core: Bar Equipment

Before you get started buying your bar equipment, you should have the exact measurements of all the rooms in your establishment and your seating capacity. This will help you come to a closer approximation of how much you'll need of certain types of equipment. Also, make sure your equipment facilitates the efficiency of your bar and your kitchen, if you serve food.

Carefully consider the design of your bar from start to finish. Remember the building blocks you played with as a kid? Well, designing your bar is like trying to fit all your blocks into a defined area. On top of that, each building block has to perform a certain function. With your bar, you not only have to consider your available space—you have to consider the bartenders' and servers' work flow as well as customer traffic. You want to get equipment that

Smart Tip

Top-notch bar equipment will meet the standards set by the National Sanitation Foundation. When you're shopping for bar equipment, look for the foundation's seal of approval. The seal practically guarantees that the equipment will meet health department codes.

will make your business as efficient as possible so your guests can get fast, friendly service from your employees.

For certain types of equipment, such as ice makers, you'll need to calculate the volume of output vs. your seating capacity and how busy you expect to be during peak hours. Your equipment vendors can give you this kind of information for all your equipment. Keep in mind that you want your business to grow, and you don't want to outgrow your equipment too quickly. Also, allow for the possibility that the manufacturer might inflate the output rating a little bit to clinch the sale.

Most bars have three different sections: the front bar, the back bar, and the under bar. The front bar is where your customers will sit. The back bar has your liquor shelves that display premium liquors, your reserve liquor cabinets, and your beer coolers. Some bars also use an over bar for additional glassware and liquor storage. The under bar is where pipes and production equipment are stored.

The Front Bar: For Your Guests

With your front bar, you'll choose your seating, bar tops, and bar fronts. These buying decisions should revolve around both cost and atmosphere—what kind of feeling you want your décor to convey. You can expect to pay anywhere from $100 to $500 per foot for a custom-made bar—unless, of course, there's a bar builder in the family. It is also possible to get bars used, if you can find some that fit your concept. You should calculate about 24 inches for each person sitting at the bar.

Your chairs can also add to your décor. Remember to keep your concept at the forefront of all your front bar purchases because this is what your customers will see. Bar stools can cost anywhere from $75 to $100 each for a standard bar stool to $400 for a custom-made stool. Lounge chairs fall into the same basic price range as bar stools, depending on the style, fabric, and design.

The Back Bar And Under Bar: For Your Bartenders

The back bar and under bar are where all the behind-the-scenes action happens. In some ways, it's the backstage area for your bar's show. The back bar displays your premium liquor bottles. It can also be the place for refrigerators, the cash register system, glass and liquor storage, beer taps, and other drink machines, such as coffee or espresso machines.

The under bar is the area of the bar where your bartenders will do most of their work, and the part your guests can't see from the front. You want to position all your back bar and under bar equipment so your bartenders can do their jobs using the least amount of movement possible. You don't want them to have to run back and forth to get what they need to make drinks. Try to keep everything they need within arm's reach. Your bartenders' work environment will include sinks, ice bins, cocktail stations,

Too Much or Not Enough?

Equipping your bar without knowing exactly how much traffic you'll have and how much they'll drink can be a bit daunting. You'll find a ton of bar equipment options, so you'll need a way to whittle down your choices. Ask yourself these 10 questions when you're making your purchasing (or leasing) decisions so you'll wind up with the right equipment for your bar:

1. Will it improve the production or service of the bar?
2. Will it meet your expectations for speed, volume, and quality?
3. Will it fit in with the concept of your bar and match the other equipment?
4. What type of warranty does it have?
5. Will it fit in the space you've allotted in your design?
6. Is it sanitary and easy to clean?
7. Is there added cost for installation and/or hookup?
8. Will it stand up to the use and abuse of your staff and/or customers?
9. Is it safe and easy to operate?
10. Does it give you room for your business to grow?

beer taps, storage cabinets, refrigerated cabinets (for beer and glasses), a mixer and blender stand, and a waste receptacle.

The bartenders' back bar work space should be about 30 inches high and about 18 to 24 inches deep. The length will depend on the maximum number of bartenders you want to have behind the bar and the length of the bar itself. Each cocktail station should include an ice bin, liquor bottle wells, a speed rack (also known as a "rail") for easy access to frequently used bottles, a garnish tray, a soda/mixer gun, and any other mixers they might need, such as Bloody Mary mix. Always keep your expected volume in mind when you're deciding on the size and capacity of your back bar and under bar. Then multiply it by 30 percent to allow for growth.

You may also consider a number of "gun" options besides your soda gun. You can also use

Smart Tip

Tip...

Look for equipment that's easy to clean. Stainless-steel equipment not only cleans up easily, but it's durable and resists mildew-causing bacteria. You don't want to buy equipment that makes it easy for your employees to skimp on the cleaning process and bring down your health code ratings.

a wine gun and a liquor gun. The placement of your guns is vital to your bartenders' efficiency. If your bartender is right-handed, he'll want the soda/mixer gun on the left so he or she can pour from bottles from the right. Similarly, if you have a liquor gun, you'll want that on the right as well. Wine guns can be placed on either side since they're generally used less frequently. (Your higher-caliber wines will be in bottles.)

Since your soda guns will need a mixture of syrup and carbonation, you'll need some under bar space to house the carbon dioxide lines and/or tank. You can opt to run the lines to a tank in a back room, too. Generally, your soda/mixer guns will include water, your chosen brand of cola, 7UP or Sprite, ginger ale, soda water, tonic, collins mix, and sweet and sour mix. You can also choose to use canned or bottled mixers, which give better quality but sacrifice storage space and the bartender's speed and efficiency.

Glassware

When picking a style of glassware, you want to keep your customers' expectations in mind as well as your own image and concept. Your glassware should match the overall décor. Glassware breaks. It's part of the business. It's fragile, and you'll have to replace it often. The size of your glassware will also determine the strength of your drinks; it affects the amount of liquor vs. mixer. It's also a vital factor in your drink-pricing decisions.

You can use glassware as a marketing tool for certain drinks. If a drink comes in a fancy glass, it gives an upscale appearance, and as a result, you can give it a higher price. Some glasses look and feel heavier, which gives the customer the illusion that the drink is bigger than it actually is. Other glasses have flared inner containers, which also make it look like a larger drink. You can even use your glassware to enhance a fun, casual, and bargain-priced bar. Your glassware can be a magical tool; use it wisely!

The glassware you choose should also be easy to clean. If you don't have a lot of storage space, you should consider stackable glasses. Or you can get racks that hang stemmed glassware over the bar from the base. Here's a list of questions to ask yourself when picking out your bar's glassware:

- Does the style match the concept of my bar?
- Is the size of the glass appropriate for the quantity of liquor I want to use in the drinks?
- Is the design durable enough that they won't have to be replaced too often?
- How much will the glasses be used? (Brewpubs don't necessarily need champagne glasses!)
- Will the cost fit my budget?

If your bar will serve beer, wine, and liquor beverages, you'll want to have different kinds of glasses for various drinks. Try to keep some consistency in the style of

How Many Glasses?

Depending on the type of drinks your bar serves and the size of your bar, your glassware stock will vary. Here's a sample behind-the-bar inventory for an establishment that serves about 50 to 75 people every two hours.

Glass	Size	Inventory
Pint glass	16 ounce	48
Beer mug	10–12 ounce	48
Pilsner glass	9–11 ounce	36
Sport mug	25 ounce	24
Bucket	15 ounce	48
Rocks glass	7–9 ounce	48
Highball	5 ounce	36
Shot glass	1 ounce	24
Wine	8.5–10.5 ounce	24
Champagne	5.5 ounce	12
Martini	5 ounce	24
Soft drink/tall mixed drink	10–12 ounce	36
Cordial	1 ounce	12
Sherry	2 ounce	12
Brandy snifter	12 ounce	12
Tulip glass	14–16 ounce	24
Margarita	5.5 ounce	24
Coffee mug	8 ounce	12

your glassware. You don't want to send out mixed-image messages by having both fancy and plain glasses, or clear and colored, or extra large and extra small. As always, keep your bar's concept at the forefront of your mind when making all your purchasing decisions.

Deciding how many glasses to buy is another issue altogether. For an idea, read "How Many Glasses?" above.

Equipping the Back of the House

Beyond the bar, you'll need some other equipment to run your business. If you plan to serve food, you'll need kitchen equipment. The size and amount will depend on what kind of food you serve and the size of your menu. Talk to several different

▲

restaurant equipment vendors to determine the type of equipment you need and the cost. Once you have your list, you can apply the same theories as you did with your bar equipment, as far as buying new, leasing, or buying used. If you have a kitchen manager or chef, he or she can make a world of difference in helping you pick out the right equipment. For an extensive list of the equipment you may need, turn to page 81.

You'll also need basic office equipment to run your bar. Most of the owners we talked to had a computer, laser printer, multiline telephones, a fax machine, copier, a safe, and either cash registers or computer registers. One bar owner also had security cameras placed throughout the establishment to help prevent theft and burglaries.

Equipment Checklist and Worksheet

Since every bar will need equipment to match its specialty, we've come up with some basics every bar will need, along with some other specialty items you might have in your bar. Of course, we can't include it all! It's up to you to decide what will and won't work for you. You can also talk to your equipment suppliers ahead of time to work out a more defined shopping list for your bar. Even if you decide to buy used equipment, a supplier can help you figure out what you need before you start writing all those checks.

Don't forget to fill in the price for your budget!

- ❏ Glassware $_____
- ❏ Compartment sinks $_____
- ❏ Drain boards $_____
- ❏ Speed racks (also known as "rails") $_____
- ❏ Overhead glass rack $_____
- ❏ Glass chiller/mug froster $_____
- ❏ Beer taps and dispensing system $_____
- ❏ Cooler for beer kegs $_____
- ❏ Freezer (for ice cream) $_____
- ❏ Ice bins $_____
- ❏ Ice machine $_____
- ❏ Ice pick $_____
- ❏ Ice scoops $_____
- ❏ Liquor wells $_____
- ❏ Dishwasher $_____
- ❏ Storage racks $_____
- ❏ Display shelves $_____
- ❏ Storage cabinets $_____
- ❏ Soda/mixer guns $_____
- ❏ Condiment trays $_____
- ❏ Tongs $_____
- ❏ Plastic juice containers/dispensers $_____
- ❏ Coffee maker $_____
- ❏ Cream dispensers $_____
- ❏ Sugar and spice dispensers $_____
- ❏ Espresso machine $_____

Equipment Checklist and Worksheet, continued

- ❏ Blenders $_____
- ❏ Refrigerators $_____
- ❏ Ashtrays $_____
- ❏ Straw and napkin holders $_____
- ❏ Serving trays $_____
- ❏ Wood muddler $_____
- ❏ Funnels $_____
- ❏ Bar spoons $_____
- ❏ Pour spouts $_____
- ❏ Beer bottle openers $_____
- ❏ Can openers $_____
- ❏ Corkscrews $_____
- ❏ Ice buckets $_____
- ❏ Floor mats $_____
- ❏ Pouring mats $_____
- ❏ Trash cans $_____
- ❏ Check holders $_____

Office and Related Equipment

- ❏ Computer $_____
- ❏ Laser printer $_____
- ❏ Calculators $_____
- ❏ Fax machine $_____
- ❏ Copier $_____
- ❏ Telephones $_____
- ❏ Cash registers $_____
- ❏ Safe $_____
- ❏ Credit card system $_____

Miscellaneous Equipment

- ❏ Cleaning equipment (brooms, mops, etc.) $_____
- ❏ Fire extinguishers $_____
- ❏ First-aid kit $_____
- ❏ Knives $_____

8

How Many Bottles on the Wall?: Inventory

Once you have your equipment in place and you're just about ready to open, you can start working with your suppliers to get your startup inventory. That means it's time to finalize your drink and food menus.

What's On Tap?

First, start with your beverage selection. If you're a beer bar or brewpub, this will be quick and easy. You probably already have a pretty good idea what you're going to offer on your drink menu. If you add wine, then you have a little more work to do. And if you serve liquor, then you'll need to pull out a piece of paper and start doing the inventory!

Your beverage selection, combined with your pricing and presentation, will have a significant effect on your business and your success. You want to get it right, right? So let's get down to business. First, pull out your mission statement and your market research. What do your customers like to drink? Most bars that offer beer, wine, and liquor carry three or four different levels of liquor quality.

The first and the lowest quality is called "well" liquor. It's the liquor your bartenders will serve when a guest doesn't specify a brand. For example, they may order a "vodka collins" or a "scotch and soda." These are called well drinks because the bottles sit in the bartender's well in the workstation, away from customers' direct view.

If a guest orders a specific brand by name, this is referred to as a "call" brand liquor. These liquors are generally the next level of quality. It's also the next level of pricing. You can either keep the bottles on speed racks in the bartender's work area or on the shelves in the back bar where customers can see them.

Finally, you can have "premium" and "superpremium" liquors. (No, we're not talking about gasoline here, but they can fuel the success of your business!) These are the high-priced brands of liquor that aren't ordered as frequently as the call brands. Again, your premium and superpremium liquors will have an even higher price than call brands and should always be placed prominently on a shelf in the back bar.

So which brands should be call and which should be premium? That is entirely up to you. You can start with a basic structure and change it along the way as you get more of an idea of what your customers are drinking and how much they value certain brands. Remember that your selection will add to your first impression when you open. Your selection of brands will tell your customers what you think of them, and they're going to compare prices and selection with your competitors.

You should also keep a close eye on your inventory throughout the life of your business. You don't want to buy too much, or you'll be wasting your money. You also don't want to buy

Smart Tip

Tip...

Your distributors and suppliers are in business just like you. You should expect the same courtesy, respect, and service from them that your customers expect from you. Don't be afraid to be direct and tell them what you want right upfront, but don't push them over the line so they don't want to do business with you, either.

too little, because then your customers may not get what they order. Walking the tightrope is the name of the game when it comes to inventory in the food and beverage industries. If you don't manage your inventory properly, it can mean the end of your business—even if you do everything else right.

To get an idea of the types and brands of liquors you need to buy, take a look at the "Startup Inventory Checklist" on page 86.

Creating Bar Cuisine

By now, you should have a pretty good idea what kind of food you want to serve in your bar—if you want to serve food at all. If you're going to serve sandwiches or appetizers, you can probably start selecting your food inventory without a chef. However, if you plan to serve more complex lunch and/or dinner entrees, you should wait to finalize your menu and make startup food inventory decisions until you have your chef on board.

Once you open your doors, constantly review your food menu. Unlike your liquor inventory, your food inventory will have a very short shelf life. If a particular item isn't selling well and is simply going to waste, you should know that you need to cut your losses and take it off the menu immediately.

Your food wholesalers, sometimes also known as purveyors, may seriously impact the success or failure of your food sales business. Most suppliers want to keep their customers, so they provide quality food and timely deliveries. However, if they suspect you don't know the business very well, they may try to take advantage of you. Be sure to check the quality of every order and all incoming invoices very carefully. If you have a kitchen staff, your lead cook or chef will most likely deal with your food suppliers.

Beware!

Throughout the life of your business, make sure you pay your suppliers in a timely manner. Even if you have an excellent personal rapport with them, the almighty dollar still goes a long way toward developing and maintaining credibility. Your suppliers can be great assets, but you don't want to get on their bad sides!

In addition to quality, you want to keep close tabs on food inventory. Ordering too much of a particular item will cost you profits, but ordering too little will cost you customer service. You'll inevitably run out of certain menu items every once in a while. To prevent further problems, make sure the communication between the kitchen staff and wait staff is smooth and efficient. If you have run out of something on the menu, the servers should know it before they take a customer's order for that item.

Working with Suppliers

One key to success in the bar business is developing a good relationship with your suppliers and

Startup Inventory Checklist

The brands of alcohol you carry in your bar will vary depending on what your customers are drinking at any given time. Just like fashion trends, certain liquors go through popularity trends. What's a hot-selling drink now may not fly out the door in six months. You need to keep a close eye on what's selling and what's not. Here's a sample liquor inventory checklist to help get you started. Write the brand names you expect to carry in the blanks.

Well Liquors
- ❑ Vodka
- ❑ Scotch
- ❑ Gin
- ❑ Bourbon
- ❑ Rum (light and dark)
- ❑ Tequila
- ❑ Brandy/Cognac
- ❑ Coffee liqueur
- ❑ Triple sec

Other Brands
- ❑ _____
- ❑ _____
- ❑ _____

Call or Premium Liquors

Vodka
- ❑ Absolut
- ❑ Grey Goose
- ❑ Ketel One
- ❑ Skyy
- ❑ Smirnoff
- ❑ Stolichnaya

Flavored Vodka
- ❑ Absolut Citron
- ❑ Absolut Mandarin
- ❑ Absolut Peppar
- ❑ Smirnoff Green Apple Twist
- ❑ Stolichnaya Orange
- ❑ Stolichnaya Raspberry

Blended Scotch
- ❑ Chivas Regal
- ❑ Cutty Sark
- ❑ Dewar's
- ❑ J & B
- ❑ Johnny Walker-Black
- ❑ Johnny Walker-Red

Single-Malt Scotch
- ❑ Glenlivet

Gin
- ❑ Beefeater
- ❑ Bombay
- ❑ Tanqueray

Bourbon
- ❑ Jim Beam
- ❑ Maker's Mark
- ❑ Seagram "7"
- ❑ Wild Turkey 101

Rum
- ❑ Bacardi 151
- ❑ Bacardi Amber
- ❑ Bacardi Limon
- ❑ Bacardi Silver
- ❑ Captain Morgans
- ❑ Meyers
- ❑ Mount Gay

Tequila
- ❑ Cabo Wabo
- ❑ Jose Cuervo 1800

Startup Inventory Checklist, continued

- ❏ Jose Cuervo Especial
- ❏ Sauza Conmemorativo

Blended whiskey
- ❏ Seagram "7"

Tennessee whiskey
- ❏ Jack Daniels Old No. 7 Black Label

Irish whiskey
- ❏ Jamison
- ❏ Old Bushmills

Canadian whiskey
- ❏ C.C.
- ❏ Crown Royal
- ❏ Seagram's V.O.

Cognac
- ❏ Courvoisier
- ❏ Hennessy
- ❏ Martell
- ❏ Remy Martin

Cordials
- ❏ Amaretto
- ❏ Annisette
- ❏ Apple Jack
- ❏ Apricot Brandy
- ❏ B & B
- ❏ Bailey's Irish Cream
- ❏ Blackberry Brandy
- ❏ Blue Caraçao

- ❏ Campari
- ❏ Chambord
- ❏ Cointreau
- ❏ Cream de Banana
- ❏ Cream de Cacao
- ❏ Cream de Menthe
- ❏ Cream de Nova
- ❏ Drambuie
- ❏ Frangelico
- ❏ Galliano
- ❏ Godiva
- ❏ Goldschläger
- ❏ Grand Marnier
- ❏ Jägermeister
- ❏ Kahlua
- ❏ Malibu
- ❏ Midori
- ❏ Ouzo
- ❏ Pernod
- ❏ Peppermint Schnapps
- ❏ Rumpleminz
- ❏ Sambuca
- ❏ Sloe Gin
- ❏ Southern Comfort
- ❏ Tia Maria
- ❏ Triple Sec
- ❏ Tuaca
- ❏ Vermouth

Beer
- ❏ Amstel Light
- ❏ Bass Ale
- ❏ Budweiser
- ❏ Bud Light
- ❏ Corona
- ❏ Dos Equis
- ❏ Guinness

- ❏ Heineken
- ❏ Michelob
- ❏ Miller
- ❏ Miller Lite
- ❏ _____
- ❏ _____
- ❏ _____
- ❏ _____

Startup Inventory Checklist, continued

House Wine
- ❏ Blush wine
- ❏ White
- ❏ Red
- ❏ Sparkling wine

Other Wines
- ❏ _____
- ❏ _____

- ❏ _____
- ❏ _____
- ❏ _____
- ❏ _____
- ❏ _____
- ❏ _____
- ❏ _____
- ❏ _____
- ❏ _____

distributors. They can help you in many, many ways. They can tell you what liquor or beer is hot on the market at any given time. They can give you general information about what's selling at other bars in the area. And they can work with you to make sure you order just the right amount for your particular business. You also want to find the right suppliers to match your business. Look at all your options. Here is a list of ten questions you can ask yourself as you're shopping for suppliers and distributors:

1. What brands do they carry?
2. Are they popular brands?
3. Do their products fit your bar's concept?
4. What are their payment terms?
5. Do they offer any discounts?
6. Do they provide any assistance with promotions? What kind?
7. How often do they make deliveries?
8. Do they require a minimum purchase?
9. If they are not a local supplier, what is their freight policy?
10. How do they prioritize order processing? First come, first served? Or larger orders first?

The Quantity Question

Now that you've located the suppliers you want to work with, it's time to decide what and how much you should buy. Find out how often you can expect deliveries (the average delivery schedule is once a week). You want to make sure you don't run out of anything before your next delivery arrives. However, when you first start out, you may not correctly gauge the popularity of certain beverages. During the first six months, you should monitor your inventory and sales very closely to make sure you're ordering enough of the popular items and not too much of the less popular items. If you end up with too much of a certain liquor, consider running a special promotion to get rid of overstock. You could try a two-for-one special, give bottles away to special regular customers as "thank you" gifts, or give them away as door prizes. Always check your local laws before running any liquor promotions,

> ## Smart Tip _Tip..._
>
> Keep your backup bottles arranged by type of alcohol. Then ask your managers to memorize the par for each of the liquor sections behind the bar and in the speed racks so they can do periodic spot checks throughout their shifts. This will call attention to missing bottles or liquor that's brought in illegally.

though. Giving away bottles of liquor—or even offering drinks at a discount price—isn't always allowed.

Remember: The cost of your inventory means more than just the amount of alcohol you buy. It also translates into storage space in your bar, and money that's tied up in inventory could be used to support your business in other better ways.

Generally, you want to buy liquor by the case (12 1-liter bottles per case). Your back bar will most likely be designed to hold liter- or quart-size bottles. These sizes are also the easiest for a bartender to handle. However, if you're using an automatic dispensing system, you might want to get 1.75-liter bottles instead to save on cost and restocking frequency.

If you find that you're not using a particular type of liquor enough to justify buying a case, you can talk to your supplier about buying a split case or a mixed case. This option costs a bit more per bottle than a regular case, but it will save you space and probably money in the long run.

You'll want to buy plenty of your well liquors and beer, and restock your house wine at least once a week. Specialty wines can be purchased by the case once a month and some as infrequently as twice a year. Keep in mind that liquor doesn't go bad, but some wine and beer can spoil.

When you've established your regular inventory, you'll need to create a plan for inventory control. We'll cover daily, monthly, and annual inventory control in more detail in Chapter 9.

"Par" for the Course

Once you have your startup inventory in place, you'll want to figure out your par for each type of liquor. Par, which isn't an acronym, is the number of backup bottles

Liquor Stock Control Form

Date _____

Bartender _____

Bar Station _____

Liquor Type/Brand	Par	Number of Bottles Used
Number of Bottles Taken from Stock		

Manager's Signature _____

you need behind the bar to keep from running out of well- and call-brand liquors in the course of one business day. This number can change any time you want it to, and you should review it periodically to make sure you're "on par."

It may take a while before you start to figure out what your par is for every type of liquor. For example, let's say you decide to use the number of bottles used at each bar on the busiest night of the year as your ongoing par. You should then set a par amount for each brand of liquor in your well brands, call brands, and frequently used cordials. You should always have a minimum of at least one backup bottle for each of these sections.

Once you've reached a reliable par behind each bar, your bartenders and barbacks should never have to go to the storeroom while you're open. As part of bartenders' closing (or opening) duties, they'll need to make sure the bar is at "full par" for the next business day. If you have a large bar or club, you might also want your bartenders to check the par between shifts.

Some bars keep a watchful eye on their inventories (and their staffs) by requiring their bartenders to fill out a liquor stock control form. When it's time to restock the bar, the bartender puts all the empty bottles on top of the bar. They write down the total number of empty bottles on the form and give it to the manager. The manager checks the bottles against the form and gives the replacements to the bartender. This process makes it easier to keep track of inventory and discover missing bottles. You'll find a "Liquor Stock Control Form" on the previous page.

From Dawn to Dawn: Operations

You've heard the term "operation" many times in reference to your bar-related business. Calling your bar an operation fits because of how much operating it takes to keep it running. Someone will have to mind the store every minute your doors are open, and your place will need some sort of monitoring during the off-hours to prevent vandalism or break-ins.

This chapter provides valuable resources and suggestions on how to successfully run your establishment on a daily basis. You'll begin by choosing the systems, setting the controls, and navigating the flow of your business from open to close. Then, you'll need to sharpen and use your ability to recognize cracks in the operation.

Many compare running your own business to raising a child. If this is true, then a smooth-running, problem-free, profit-making bar compares to parenting a happy, well-adjusted, self-assured teenager preparing for adulthood. But don't worry, the bumps in the road hold the best lessons. And as with parenting, you succeed with consistency and concern instead of rigidity and blame.

Rest Peacefully

Have you ever tossed and turned all night trying to get to sleep? Have you suffered from the nagging feeling you've forgotten to do something—turn off the stove or lock the back door? If so, you've probably found ways to deal with your uneasiness.

When you begin your career as an entrepreneur, you'll likely battle pestering little things that seemingly morph into huge headaches at a moment's notice. These little problems can come from anywhere. You'll encounter things like tardiness of your staff members, dishwashing machine breakdowns, dirty bathrooms, your produce delivery arriving during your dinner rush (for which you need the produce), and computer troubles. You can't predict what problems will confront you tomorrow, but you can prepare yourself and your staff to deal with just about anything by setting the groundwork and promoting communication and safety.

The Road to Success

The groundwork you lay to operate your bar includes the systems you use to track liquor and food. How much does the customer owe the server/bartender? Also, what liquor and food do you sell the most? The systems you choose depend on the type and size of bar you have.

A computer system can keep track of all your sales—right down to the point of how much you've sold of each type of product. If you decide your operation warrants the investment needed to set up a high-tech system, make

Dollar Stretcher

Thoroughly inspect any cash register system you consider for your business. Be realistic about its ease of use and justify its cost. Try to visualize how well the system will work when the people using it are rushed. Even a "small investment" can hurt you if you have to scrap the whole thing and buy a different system.

sure you understand the ins and outs of the computer. Will you need to have a separate machine to process credit cards, or will the computer handle it? Make sure at least one person on your staff has a thorough knowledge of your computer and/or

---

Show Me the Money

You'll have to employ some sort of system for ordering and paying. You have many to choose from, and whichever one you choose will most likely bring lots of baggage with it. Here's a list of some of the systems used in this industry to pay the check, along with the pros and cons of each.

Cash-and-Carry
○ *Pro.* Since there's no ticket involved, all the server has to do is call the drink to the bartender, deliver it, and get the money for it. It's a very fast-operating system.
○ *Con.* Who rings the drink in? If there's only one register, then the bartender will most likely ring it up. If so, when does he get the money for the drink if the customer pays with a credit card?
○ *Con.* There is a high chance of theft in this system. Using cameras focused on the register could cut down on theft, but you may want to invest that money in a computer system that stops theft without surveillance.

Handwritten Tickets
○ *Pro.* It's easier to account for drinks made if they're all written down; there's organization and control of all the checks.
○ *Pro.* It's much cheaper than a computer system.
○ *Con.* With this system, there's the inability to order food and liquor from the same check.
○ *Con.* It can be time consuming, especially if your bartenders or servers have to write down each order or each round of drinks.

Computerized Tickets
○ *Pro.* This is the most efficient and effective way of communicating in a clear and concise way to the bar and the kitchen.
○ *Con.* This is the most expensive ordering system.
○ *Con.* There are many different kinds of computerized ordering systems. Generally, the expert you rely on in this area is a salesperson. If you buy a system with a lot functions you won't use, then you could be wasting money.

cash register system in case anything goes wrong. Supply this person with a pager so you can reach them in case of an emergency breakdown.

Factors to consider when choosing an accounting system include the level of sales you expect, both from alcohol and food, and the efficiency needed for your staff to operate at its full potential. Also, look for holes that your accounting system might leave open for theft at all levels, not just servers and bartenders. No one thinks they're hiring a thief. Many people who might steal if the opportunity arose don't consider themselves thieves, either, so they don't come off as such.

If you use the cash-and-carry system, where the drink is ordered by the server verbally and then paid for before the bartender or server rings it up, you might find many "forgot to ring it up" drinks, as well as a few given away for free. It's the nature of the system. If your inventory controls are so tight that you'll notice when too much has been used then you can use this system without much fear.

Communication Is Key

If you haven't trained your employees in the proper steps to take when ordering or filling an order, they won't do it correctly. Your bar business functions as a whole. For example, a guest's chicken sandwich has Dijon mustard on it instead of yellow mustard because he asked for the modification. The server understood the request and communicated the order to the kitchen. Your employees must comprehend exactly what their role is on your team and how to correctly execute their duties.

To help your lines of communication grow and stay strong, you need to keep your employees up-to-date on changes in policy and duties. We'll talk more about this in the next chapter, but you should make sure your employees know your expectations at all times to prevent confusion about responsibilities. A lot of managers don't post employee duties charts for each position or the schedule of special side-work chores. This oversight can cause holes in your team's fabric and inhibit production. If you make sure your employees have all the information they need, they can't use ignorance as an excuse, and you can prevent finger-pointing among your staff.

Getting Through Each Day

Establish a routine for yourself from the moment you walk in the door. You or your general manager may arrive before anyone else. Or, by the time you start your workday, the operation may have already started. The person who cleans the place, the person who sweeps the parking lot, your prep cooks, and other employees have already started their days before the first customer walks in the door. From the moment the decision maker steps on the premises, whether alone or not, they should keep a watchful eye on any inconsistencies or errors. They shouldn't only observe any problems but determine the possible causes of them.

By establishing a routine for yourself, you can intimately familiarize yourself with the way things should be running. When you get to work, take a tour of the facility. Any lapse in cleaning or closing duties from the night before will jump out at you. Take note of any misdeed and discuss the inconsistency with the employee responsible. The politically correct name for this procedure is "counseling" the employee. Generally, the closing staff will have to check out with the manager on duty, which means your daily tour should rarely cause you this irritation.

As part of your routine, adjust the lights to their proper illumination, set the heater or air conditioner early so your guests have a comfortable environment, and then go to the office where the phone messages, the log book, and the daily schedule will start your day rolling.

Settling Into Your Office

If your schedule allows it, you should get to work a couple hours before you open to take care of emergency situations, like equipment failure or an employee calling in sick. You can also use this time to interview potential employees, accept deliveries (if you don't have a kitchen manager), and count liquor inventory (if you don't have a bar manager). Most of all, this time allows you to catch up with the endless stream of daily information that bombards all bar managers and owners.

In your office, you should have a managerial log book or diary. This book transfers information from one shift supervisor to the next. You and your managers should write down anything from customers finding metal staples in their salad to actions taken with a disorderly drunk. Communications between shifts help tremendously when it comes to steering a smooth-sailing ship.

The log book entry from the previous shift manager can also inform you of other news, such as inventory or cash shortages, "counseling" sessions they had with employees, and general reminders of things you have to do. If you're short on supplies on a Sunday morning, you can call one of your opening staff members to see if they can stop by the store for you on their way in. During the course of your day, remember to write down the things you want the other managers to know in the log book.

Bright Idea

During your opening walk-through of the facility, visually inspect your kitchen and bar equipment to make sure the pieces were cleaned and replaced properly. This glance pays big dividends if you prevent the malfunction and possible breakdown of the machine.

Don't expect yourself to remember to tell them. You'll have hundreds of things to remember, which is why you have the book in the first place.

Next, while you're still in your office, go to your safe and count out the necessary banks for the shift. If you have a full-time bookkeeper, this would fall under his or her responsibilities. Generally, your servers will carry their own banks or make change out of the bartender's till. The typical starting bank for each cash register is $200 to $300. A standard breakdown for a $200 till is: $30 in tens, $50 in fives, $75 in ones, $30 in quarters, $10 in dimes, $4 in nick-els and $1 in pennies. You should make change orders every weekday when you go to the bank. Don't forget to load up on extra change for those times when the bank will be closed, such as holidays and weekends. When placing the banks in the registers, you or your bookkeeper should make sure last night's shift sales have been cleared out so the machine is ready to register today's sales.

Before leaving the office, you can visualize the shift ahead by estimating the volume of business and looking at who will be working and when they're due to start. If you operate with a handwritten ticket system, you can document the ticket numbers for each server and bartender at this time.

Beware!
Even though it's a good idea to keep your inventory low because it represents cash, it can cost you a lot if you run out of a popular liquor due to under-ordering. To prevent this, you can sometimes make emergency inventory purchases to get you through until your regular delivery day.

Open for Business

To reaffirm your commitment to your customers, you should open on time every day. Your opening staff must show up on time and have the place ready before you open the doors. When your bartenders, servers, host, and office staff start to arrive, they can help answer phones, and you can go back to the office to look over the sales and inventory checklists from yesterday. This is also a good time to catch up on any other paperwork you have to do or start planning for your next big promotional event. Just before you open the doors, take one more look around to double check prepared-ness—not out of distrust of your employees, but to reinforce to yourself your own ultimate responsibility for everything. If you act interested in perfection, your staff will know you're serious, and they'll follow your example.

Sometimes you'll have a server, bartender, busser, or barback who doesn't show up for a shift or shows up in no shape to work. If you schedule on-call shifts and it's not too late to activate them, you may have an easy fix. Otherwise, rearrange the worksta-tions to accommodate the fact that you have one less employee, and fill in yourself wherever you can to help compensate for the missing piece. You can offer customers another drink when their server is too busy to catch the order, you can run food from the kitchen, and you can do a million other little things that will help your team thrive, even under tough circumstances. Then, when the fury of the shift is over, get to the bottom of why it happened and try to solve it for the future.

Maintaining Guest Relations

A crucial and sometimes very difficult aspect of managing a bar is dealing with rude, overbearing customers who seem like they're always cranky and dissatisfied. Here's one example of how to deal with a complaining patron: You overhear a server ask her customer if he would like another drink. He answers gruffly that she didn't put any alcohol in the first one, so why should he pay for another one? Your server assures him the bartender pours a full two ounces for each drink (or whatever your standard pour is), yet he still complains. To soothe the situation for your server, you go over and talk to the customer, reaffirming what your server said.

To appease the gentleman, you instruct the bartender to put a little more alcohol in his drink or do it yourself. If you feel a customer is complaining only to see how much he can get for free, don't appease him any further. Instead, inform him he should order a double if he wants more than the standard pour. If you lose your composure, no one wins. The stiffness—or lack thereof—of a drink (or any other customer concern) is no reason to get upset and lose the respect of your regular customers and/or your staff. Remember, this is a public place. Never allow your employees to argue with a customer, either. Make sure they know to get a manager involved with any dispute before they do anything they may have to apologize for later. Show them they can lean on you and your managers in difficult situations.

When dealing with guests' problems, maintain eye contact in a respectful, attentive way, and listen to their problem. Whether you believe them or not, you have to listen, but in this business, you don't have to give in just because they are customers. For example, if a guest says he paid his $14 check with a $100 bill, but your bartender says it was a $50 bill, you don't have to give the customer $50 extra just because they demand it. Of course, if the bartender doesn't have any $100 bills in his or her till, you already know the right answer. If that's not the case, simply take the guest's name and telephone number, and at the end of the shift, double- and triple-check to see if the drawer is $50 over. If it is, you'll let the customer know and give it back. Keep in mind that you'll be dealing with customers who

Bright Idea

Keep a lost-and-found box in a safe place. If a customer calls saying they lost a personal item, have them describe it in detail (including its contents). If a wallet or purse are claimed, make sure you give it to the right person—you can ask them personal questions found on their driver's license.

are drinking alcohol, and as a result, the customer may not always be right. Use your best judgment to decide how to handle complaints and other guest-related situations.

To help you run your operation smoothly and successfully, pay close attention to what's happening around you at all times. Whether you're in the front of the house or the back, you can read frustration on the faces of your employees and your customers. If you sense something's wrong, check into it. It never hurts to ask if everything is OK.

Preventing Theft

Unfortunately, one of the biggest things you have to watch out for during the course of your workday is theft. Customers leaving without paying the check, passing counterfeit money, or stealing your empty beer mugs are all potential problems you'll face, but they pale in comparison to the damage your employees can do by stealing from you. Back-of-the-house theft—that of food and food products—pales by comparison to what your bartenders can get away with if they're so inclined and unsupervised.

Not all bartenders steal, but enough of them do that some surveillance professionals make their entire living watching bartenders. Bob Johnson, CEO of the Beverage Management Institute in Clearwater, South Carolina, estimates in his book *The Disgusting Practice of Bartender Theft* (BobTheBarGuy.com) that about 70 to 80 percent of bartenders rip off their employers. Many otherwise morally strong bartenders steal in some way or another because the ease of doing so is overwhelming to the point that they can rationalize it. The most common form of bartender theft is giving free drinks to their friends and favorite customers. The bartenders' tip jar can fill up with money generated by the free drinks they give away. Customers often tip the bartender the same amount they would have paid for the drink.

Many bar managers who suspect employee theft hire spotters who pose as customers in the bar to come in and catch the thief in the act, then report it to the manager. If you choose to use spotters, always check out their credentials first. There are many spotters who work with local security companies and don't know how a bar operates. If a spotter hasn't worked as a bartender or server before, he or she might mistake a harmless gesture as an overt act of theft. Also, experienced bartenders move very quickly and therefore pose problems for the untrained eye. If you use spotters, tell your employees about your use of undercover shoppers. It should serve as a strong deterrent to theft.

Keep a Close Count

In addition to the universal tricks your employees can use to steal from you, watch out for holes in your systems. A glaring example is the cash-and-carry system of

See How They Steal

In his book, *The Disgusting Practice of Bartender Theft* (BobTheBarGuy.com), Bob Johnson has identified 51 different methods bartenders use to rob you blind. Whether they steal directly from your bar or from the customers, it can ruin your bar. Here's a breakdown of the major infractions to look out for.

Stealing from Your Customers

○ *Overcharging.* A bartender takes advantage of a customer who doesn't know your prices.

○ *Short pouring.* The bartender pours half the amount of alcohol the customer ordered.

○ *Making change.* A bartender can steal some of the patrons' change by taking advantage of their intoxication and giving the wrong change. Also, a bartender or server can pass off counterfeit bills to customers.

○ *Padding the bill.* Guests who don't know your prices and have many rounds of drinks can get charged an extra couple bucks per round.

○ *Incorrect totals.* The bartender intentionally adds the check incorrectly and gives a higher total in pencil. After the guest leaves, the pencil is erased, leaving the lower actual total, and the bartender pockets the rest.

Stealing from You

○ *Outright theft.* A bartender makes a drink and either gives it away or sells it without ringing it up.

○ *Overpouring.* To ensure a hefty tip, some bartenders give regular customers heavier liquor pours.

○ *Reusing tabs.* A bartender can present his current guest with the check of a past guest who had the same thing.

○ *Payouts.* If the bartender reimburses money lost in video games or jukeboxes, they can pay out phony claims and keep the money.

○ *Personal booze.* A bartender bent on stealing may bring in his own bottle of alcohol to sell at your bar. Vodka makes a good choice for sneaking in because it can pass as water. A bartender who brings in a $10 bottle of vodka from home can earn a huge markup on it by pouring it in the bar and pocketing the money.

▲

Bright Idea

If you suspect your bartenders or servers are stealing, talk to your friends and colleagues who work in the bar business. Offer them a complimentary gift certificate if they'll come in and watch your staff for theft.

order-taking. Without a paper trail, you have a system full of holes. Less obvious examples include your method of shift transfer. Will your system register sales made while your day bartenders are changing shifts over to the night bartenders? Also, look out for misuse of your waste sheet (the log that tracks breakage and drink mistakes) and other alcohol-control devices.

How closely you monitor your inventory deeply affects your bottom line. Although we concentrate on beer, wine, and liquor, if you serve food, you should closely regulate that inventory as well. Depending on the size of your bar, you may need to complete a daily inventory to truly determine your operation's day-to-day health.

99 Bottles of Beer on the Wall

Yes, counting every bottle of beer you have in your bar every day can cause time-management problems, not to mention splitting headaches for you or your bar manager. However, these headaches, harsh as they may be, pale compared to the migraines you'll suffer trying to figure out why you sell so much beer yet your bottom line is in the red. You may buy it by the case, but you should count it by the bottle.

Just as it is your kitchen manager's responsibility to maintain proper food controls, your bar manager, even if it's you, should count the beer bottles. If you—or your manager—are off, the task should be assigned to another manager. Don't have your bartenders calculate your running inventory. They'll decipher what stock they need to fill their bar before their shift starts, but this is different. Any inventory counts should be made when the bar is closed, and none of what you're counting will be moved.

To assure consistency, count your beer bottles the same way each day. You could start with the stock you have in dry storage, then move to your cold reinforcements in the walk-in, and finish up by counting the bottled beer still at your bars. When counting the bottles still behind the bar, you should take out every bottle and put them on top of the bar before counting. Even if your bartenders are supposed to restock their coolers with a precise number of bottles, you should double check. Mistakes happen. Don't let your laziness compound their mistakes.

Smart Tip

Bottled beer costs much more than draft beer. The price you pay per bottle can exceed twice the price you pay per serving from a keg. Because of this, you should only run promotions on draft beer, not on bottled beer.

The best way to count bottled beer is to verify each brand's volume (see the "Daily Bottled Beer Inventory" below). If you know you had 300 bottles of Budweiser yesterday and you count 111 bottles today, you know you should have sold 189 bottles of Bud since yesterday's count. Most of today's computerized cash register systems will keep track of each type of beer sold. If your system doesn't specify brands, you'll need to figure out a way to track them. If you can't do this, you'll only know the number of missing bottles, which isn't ideal but better than no control at all.

Daily Bottled Beer Inventory

Domestic	Bar 1	Bar 2	Storage	Current Count	Previous Count	Usage	Sales	Variance
Brand #1								
Brand #2								
Brand #3								
Brand #4								
Brand #5								

Domestic	Bar 1	Bar 2	Storage	Current Count	Previous Count	Usage	Sales	Variance
Brand #1								
Brand #2								
Brand #3								
Brand #4								
Brand #5								

Maintaining Your Draft Flow

Controlling the flow and profit of your draft beer can be done in one of two ways. First, you could accept an estimated number for how many glasses of beer you expect to pour from each keg and monitor it. Or you could attempt to account for every droplet of beer.

When you serve a bottle of beer, you should check for two things. First, is it cold? And second, did the glass rim chip when you opened it? When you serve a draft beer, many more things can go wrong. If something does, you have to check the temperature, the CO_2 pressure, and the beer lines. Your bartenders also have to deal with the mechanics of holding the beer mug at an angle until just the right moment to produce a proper head.

Foam kills profit. No self-respecting bartender will serve a half-beer/half-head concoction, so the would-be beer flows down the sink instead of down a throat. Generally, improper CO_2 pressure causes beer to have excess foam—one common problem that occurs when the same CO_2 tank pumps the gas for regular beer and a light beer. Your CO_2 pressure should normally be between 12 and 14 pounds per square inch (PSI). However, light beer only requires 8 to 10 PSI. The extra pressure gives tremendous head to the light beer. If you have any questions, ask your beer distributor. They'll know the optimal CO_2 pressure for their beer.

Another way to prevent waste and pouring problems is to have your beer lines cleaned every two to three weeks. Some distributors will clean the lines for you. You can inquire about this when you're starting to do business with them. Clogged beer lines cause slow pouring and testy bartenders. Also, ask your draft beer distributor what temperature of beer allows for the best results in pouring.

Generally, you'll want to keep your kegs in a refrigerator separate from bottled beer, food, etc. Sometimes called the beer box, the keg cooler should be kept between 34 and 36 degrees. The beer should move along the lines and dispense through the nozzle at 38 to 40 degrees.

You may wish to buy and use a flow meter. This device enables the bar manager to monitor nearly every ounce in the keg and thus hold the bartender responsible for the beer he or she dispenses. If you use this technology, make sure you operate it yourself so you can understand its discrepancies. For example, if the CO_2 pump is off and fills the mug with foam instead of beer, does the flow meter charge the ounces?

Stat Fact

In the bar business, "soft goods" refers to straws, glassware, coasters, syrup for your soda machine, and the like. Unless you need to know exactly how many of each you've used, you don't need to inventory these products. You can just figure 2 percent of gross beverage sales goes to soft goods.

Wine Can't This Be Love?

For wine bottles, you can use the same control system as for beer bottles. To easily estimate the number of glasses left in an open bottle of wine, use the following steps. First, instruct your bartender not to open a new bottle of a specific wine before using the existing wine from another bottle. It's OK for them to have backups open, but they should partially replace the cork and leave the bottle full until needed. This will help prevent wine from spoiling and will assist your inventory endeavors. The sizes of wine bottles you use may differ. You should know how many glasses you can expect from each, and you should tell your bartenders. Just because you know how difficult it is to account for every drop of wine or beer, that shouldn't stop you from trying, and expecting your bartenders to do the same.

Controlling Your Liquor

Unlike bottled beer and wine, you don't have to count every drop of liquor your bar possesses each day. Let's face it: You won't have time to measure how many shots are left in each bottle every day. Depending on the volume of business you do, once a week or once a month will probably do fine. However, you could add greatly to your diagnostic abilities if you identify your pour-cost percentage (PC%) for liquor weekly or even daily. Your pour-cost percentage tells you how many cents you must spend on liquor to generate one dollar of liquor sales. An optimal PC% would be in the high teens.

To calculate your PC%, you must establish pars for every kind and type of liquor you keep in your bar. (Refer to Chapter 8 for information on pars.)

Use your daily liquor stock control forms (there's a blank one on page 90 in Chapter 8) to estimate your liquor usage cost. Divide this number by your liquor sales to determine your approximate nightly pour-cost percentage for liquor. For this to work, the sales you use must only reflect liquor. Most non-computerized register systems have different buttons for liquor, beer, wine, and soft drinks. Make sure your bartenders use the right ones.

The following example shows how to calculate daily pour-cost percentage:

Liquor usage cost	$769
Total liquor sales for the day	$3,243

$769 \div 3,243 = 0.2371$ (23.7% liquor pour cost)

You use the same process and formula to decide your estimated weekly pour cost. But to establish your monthly pour cost, you should use the exact numbers from counting every drop of liquor possible. Generally, you can use tenths when counting the liquor in an open bottle. Keeping up on your PC% daily and weekly—even though they can't be exact—can benefit you greatly when you have to figure out where a loss comes from. You also want to watch for trends: Is your PC% going up or down? And, if your bartenders know you follow up every day on liquor control, they may be less likely to steal from you for fear of getting caught.

So there you have it. It's all in a day's work. If you concentrate on setting the groundwork for a system that will help your employees communicate clearly with each other, put controls in place that will safeguard you and your customers from rampant theft, and keep a tight lid on your inventory, you'll be well on your way to running a smooth operation. In Chapter 10, we'll give you some tips on how to find the best employees for your bar—from the front of the house to the back. Once you find them, we'll give you some ideas on how to manage and maintain your most valuable assets . . . your people!

10

People Serving People:
Human Resources

At this point, you've learned a lot about opening your bar business. But you can toss everything you've learned into a giant garbage can if your staff leans toward "service with a snarl" instead of sincere caretaking of your guests.

It wouldn't be much of a leap to say the most important aspect of a successful bar is its personnel. From manager to busboy and bartender to dishwasher, these people will have a huge effect on how smoothly your operation runs.

In this chapter, you'll read tales of woe and wonder concerning employees. You'll get acquainted with the most challenging areas of hiring and maintaining your staff and the importance of matching your servers' personalities with your guests' expectations. We'll also give you some tools to help spot potential problems, along with some troubleshooting ideas to help you handle them.

How's the Service?

The way people feel when they're in your bar will determine whether or not they return. Bar management consultant Bob Johnson of Clearwater, South Carolina, was approached by a desperate owner who had already invested more than $1 million into his sports bar. "I'm in big trouble," the owner told Johnson. "I don't know what's going wrong, and I don't know what to do. I've got brand-new TVs. I've got copper railings. It's the most beautiful place I could possibly put together, yet I have no customers." The owner offered to treat Johnson to a free dinner and complimentary drinks if he would pose as a customer to try to figure out what was going wrong. Johnson agreed to check it out. What happened during Johnson's visit is a perfect example of how poor service can blemish a customer's experience. Here's how Johnson recounts the experience:

"We got there around 7 P.M. The hostess said, 'Dinner?' I said, 'No, I think we will sit at the bar for now.' She just pointed and said, 'It's over there.'

"As we walked to the bar, two servers passed us. They gave no eye contact, no 'Hi, how ya doin'?' and no 'Glad to see you here.'

"When we got to the bar, the bartender was involved in a conversation with a couple of employees and a customer, and she was talking and talking and talking. This went on for about a minute and a half—which is a long time to sit at a bar without somebody noticing you. She finally broke off her conversation, came over to us and asked, 'What do you want?' I said that I would have a rum and coke, and my wife would have an Amaretto sour. The bartender didn't say anything. She just turned around, made the drinks, put them in front of us, and put the tab in front of us. She didn't say a word. She just went right back to her conversation."

This story exemplifies how meaningless all your well-thought-out preparations can become if your guests aren't served properly. You can develop the best concept in the world. But if your service is slow, surly, or inept, customers won't hang around. And they won't come back.

"You could just tear the whole building down," says Johnson. "That man had a million dollars invested in his club, and what did it mean? It meant absolutely nothing. It doesn't matter what kind of bar you have. Unless your staff has the ability and personality to deal with people in a friendly, amicable way, the entire business folds up. It's all dependent on the staff you put together. That's what determines repeat business, and that's what determines success in the bar industry."

Who's on First?

Just as you wouldn't field a baseball team without employing a first baseman, you can't field your bar's kitchen without a dishwasher. You'll decide what positions you need to create and fill based on the size and scope of your operation. Every team requires members with different strengths to meet its goals. For example, if you want to be the "Home of the World's Best Margarita," then you should always have someone on staff who can expertly make your special margarita. The same goes for the specialty foods you offer. If your product is special because of its preparation or presentation, and you're not the one preparing or presenting it, then be sure those who make it know how to do it right.

However, the types of employees you'll be choosing from are pretty universal. A good way to categorize the employees in the bar industry is front of the house, back of the house, and swing.

Front-of-the-house employees include bartenders, servers, and hosts. The back of the house is made up of chefs, prep cooks, dishwashers, office staff (secretary, bookkeeper, etc.), and the maintenance staff (usually subcontracted). Swing employees are the managers, bussers, barbacks, security (where necessary), and expediters (expediters are most frequently found in larger food operations; otherwise, managers usually do the job when it's necessary).

If you're serious about opening a bar, then you already know how much work it takes. To focus solely on your sales would be a mistake—you must think about how the work will get done. Who will do it? You need to consider all the different chores your particular operation will depend on. How you structure your bar to get all these chores done is completely up to you and your managers.

The flow charts on page 110 show different ways to structure your employees. Whether you want to open a small, no-kitchen, neighborhood bar or a full-kitchen bar and grill, you can use the charts when you make your roster of employees to ensure that you've covered all your bases.

Bright Idea

Every few months, ask someone you know to come in and evaluate the service in your bar. Make sure your staff doesn't know who they are ahead of time. It takes an unbiased party to give you an accurate assessment of the type of service your customers receive.

Staff Structure with an Active Owner

This format is extremely time-consuming if you have no other managers.

Owner (with no managers)

Bartenders   Servers   Line Cooks   Security   Housekeeping

Barback/Busser   Prep Cooks

Dishwashers

Staff Structure with Limited Owner Activity

Here, the owner oversees the operation, but the general manager runs the show.

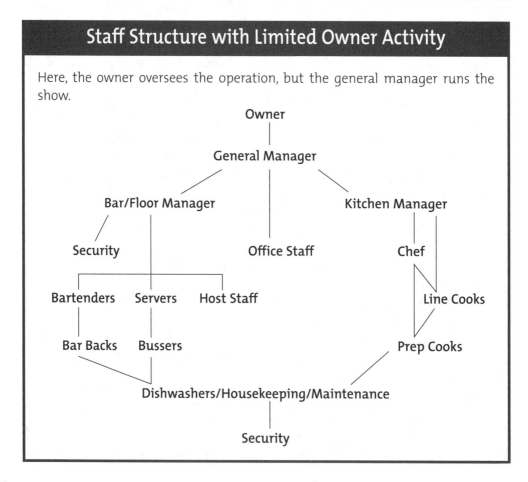

Owner

General Manager

Bar/Floor Manager   Kitchen Manager

Security   Office Staff   Chef

Bartenders   Servers   Host Staff   Line Cooks

Bar Backs   Bussers   Prep Cooks

Dishwashers/Housekeeping/Maintenance

Security

The Team Captains

Imagine having 19 different things to do right now. You would have to prioritize, delegate, and constantly double check your progress. Now imagine having to guide and help about 30 people who all have 19 things to do right now. This is what your manager has to do. Your manager must know every employee's duties and responsibilities. They must also know how to spot and develop the characteristics needed to hire and maintain a true team in your bar.

Sometimes kitchens have their own managers—a person who interviews and schedules cooks, dishwashers, prep cooks, etc. If you're a large-sized bar, you may also need a separate bar manager to oversee the bartenders, wait staff, and bussing staff. All your managers will help determine the responsibilities of your new hires and oversee their training.

It's a good idea to have one manager per shift who helps control the entire flow of the business. This one lead manager can follow all your bar's functions at the same time. But don't expect your on-duty manager to also be the shift's lead line cook or only bartender. If the manager has to take care of a guest's problem or see to an emergency, then the service will suffer. The key to having more than one manager working at one time is how well they work together toward the satisfaction of the guests.

If you're going to be active in the running of your bar, give yourself specific responsibilities, just like you would one of your managers. Gerry Kelly, the Miami club manager, warns, "A lot of people think that in the club business you get out of bed at 10 o'clock at night, and you go in and just hang out. It's not like that!" Of course, no matter how well you plan in this business, surprise duties will spring up for both you and your staff members. Occasionally, you may have to drive across town to pick up one of your employees who missed the bus. You can't possibly plan for this kind of surprise. But you can prepare for most everything else by having a solid, well-formed schedule. Your weekly schedule for the entire staff should be mapped out by either you or one of your managers.

Depending on the size of your operation, you could have up to five different titles with the word "manager" in it. Examples would include a kitchen manager, bar manager, general manager, assistant manager, floor manager (although most bars usually assign floor duties to the bar manager). If your bar only needs one manager, your candidate will need to fit the characteristics of a general manager.

Smart Tip

Tip...

Have you ever noticed that the employees at Cheers and Mel's Diner always have time to engage in serious conversation no matter how busy they are? That's not how the real world works. When you're training your servers and bartenders, make sure they know they should ask for help before their service begins to suffer.

A general manager needs the ability to smoothly run both the front and back of the house. Your general manager (or sole manager) should be someone who's as comfortable seeing to a guest's satisfaction as they are to negotiating with suppliers. They should also be comfortable dealing with employees of different expertise, background, and personality from the interview and hiring process through the day-to-day managing of personnel.

Sometimes referred to as an operations manager, your general manager must have a great deal of experience and fully understand your mission statement and the goals of your operation. If you have a larger establishment or are a less active owner, the reliability of your general manager doubles in importance. You're counting on them to not only run a clean bar but also an above-board establishment that will attract a sophisticated clientele. "I have employees who have worked for managers who didn't even do inventory," says R.C. Colvin, the bar owner in Niles, Michigan. "I can't believe some of the stories I've heard about how managers ran, or didn't run, their bars. If you look at those bars now, they're not in business anymore. Sometimes it's because they don't know how to do it, and other times I think a lot of it's just laziness." In short, you want to find a manager who holds themselves and their staff to a high standard.

Don't underestimate the importance of a good manager in this business. This is an industry where internal attitudes can completely destroy the demand for the product. It makes no difference in the shoe business if your manufacturer and your seller don't get along. Your shoe is the same. But if a bartender and cocktail server are in the middle of a horrible argument, you better believe the product and service (which is just as important) will differ exceedingly compared to a "normal" day. A good manager will spot a great majority of these types of problems before they start affecting your business.

If you're planning a small neighborhood pub, and you expect to be active in its running, you're a manager. You may choose to rule with in iron hand, or you could impress upon your staff that you're all in this together. Bob Brenlin, the Seattle bar owner, does the latter. "We're small (about 12 employees), so everybody chips in and does various things. People with larger places have much more of a structure than we do."

Smart Tip

Tip...

The people who make the best servers are smart, sincere, sensitive, and gregarious. Actors often gravitate toward bar and restaurant jobs because it's easy for them to engage the guests (just like an audience). Keep these characteristics in mind when you're deciding who to hire for your own service staff.

Front-of-the-House Staff

Let's go through some of the issues involved in making sure your front-of-the-house staff is complete and efficient:

Bartenders

As demonstrated by Bob Johnson's story at the beginning of this chapter, a bartender's attitude toward your customers heavily influences the success of the bar. Your bartender should have an affable, interactive attitude with people, and this should be reflected in how they make their drinks. Experience goes a long way, but if you're hiring for a small neighborhood bar, and you just need someone to help you out, then you can afford to hire based on the personality of the candidate alone.

Molding your bartenders is a more time-consuming proposition than finding professionals who fit your bar's concept and image. Molding takes time, training, and investment. Hiring an experienced, professional bartender is tricky, though, because their experience gives them the ability to job hop.

Then again, you may set your bar structure up to allow for revolving-door bartenders where it won't matter how quickly they leave. Of course, it would be easier and much more profitable if you could keep the same bartenders constantly working at their highest levels of efficiency and effectiveness. To do that, you'll need luck and good communication, and you'll need to run a bar that's just as much fun for your employees as it is for your customers.

Servers

Unlike a restaurant, a bar doesn't usually distinguish between cocktail servers and food servers—even if your endeavor is to have the best chicken wings in Chicago. If your establishment is bar-focused, your customers will expect your servers to have a vast knowledge of the types of liquor, mixed drinks, beer, and wine you serve, as well as what's in your food specials.

As with your bartenders, you should match the server's personality with the feeling you want to give your guests. You always want your customers to feel like guests—respected and invited. You also need to pick people who you can convince to carry the torch of your bar's concept.

Hosts

To serve your customers better, you'll want to communicate with them from the moment they contact you (via phone or in person). If you have a smaller operation, you may just have your manager answer phone calls and have your servers greet guests. Either way, a simple verbal exchange will go far in creating a rapport with people.

> **Bright Idea**
>
> Creating an atmosphere that allows your employees to speak their minds and have their ideas heard will contribute mightily to your staff's team spirit. The trick is to listen very closely and pay attention. Don't forget to periodically ask your back-of-the-house staff for input as well.

If you have a larger establishment, you might want to have a host or hostess at the door to greet and seat your guests. A good host must be able to handle having time on their hands at some points during the shift, then having many tasks to do at the same time at other points.

Additional Employees: Your operation may need a full-time bookkeeper or secretary. Or you may just need a proverbial "Gal Friday" or "Jack of All Trades." Consider combining the latter with the host position. That person could greet and seat customers during your busy hours, as well as do the daily books, keep the files, and answer the phones during off-hours.

Back-of-the-House Staff

When you and your managers strive to establish a team atmosphere among your staff, one of the most essential (and easy to break down) areas is between the front of the house and the back of the house. Of course, this only comes into play when you have a kitchen staff. If you only serve alcohol and snacks, this won't be an issue for you. Your back-of-the-house staff members don't receive tips as part of their compensation, so they will cost more in your payroll.

- *Chef/lead cook*. Besides the manager, your most instrumental person in the back of the house is your chef or lead cook.

- *Line cooks*. Your line cooks prepare the menu items under the direction of the lead cook or chef. The area of the kitchen that contains the stoves, ovens, and other cooking equipment is usually defined as the "line."

- *Prep cooks*. They cut, chop, clean, and anything else that helps prepare the dishes you serve. Preparing food for the public is a major responsibility. If it's not done right, it can do serious damage to your business. Your cooks are on the front lines of health and safety issues when it comes to the food you serve. They not only need to pass a test issued by your local health department officials, but they have to continually follow the rules afterward.

- *Dishwashers*. In a bar or restaurant, dishwashers often do more than rinse off dishes and guide them through a machine. They're often charged with taking out the trash, cleaning the parking lot, and sweeping and mopping the floors. Dishwashers generally receive the lowest pay of the nontipped employees in this industry.

Front and Back: Swing

Some members of your staff will "swing" back and forth from the front and back of the house. Of course, managers fall into this category, and so do bussers and barbacks.

These positions help pace your business. Let's explain the difference between a busser and a barback.

- *Barback*. A barback's primary responsibility is to keep the bar stocked, clean, and user-friendly for the bartender. You might think of your barbacks as bartenders' assistants. Your bartenders should give their barbacks a percentage of their tips. This is called a "tip-out" or "tipping out."
- *Busser*. The busser's primary responsibility is taking care of the tables. Bussers are servers' assistants. They clear and clean tables and get them ready for the next customers. The busser also works as an extension of the servers. If servers don't have time to get refills or other little things for their customers, their bussers can jump in to help. Your servers will tip out the bussers as well.

In smaller bars, the barback and busser may be the same person. As a result, this person will work for the bartenders and servers at the same time. This can turn into a tricky undertaking but ends up being quite profitable for the person who's doing both jobs since both the bartenders and servers tip them out.

Setting a Salary Cap

Your budget will go a long way in determining what you should pay your managers and back-of-the-house staff. Managers' salaries may vary as much as the managers themselves. A manager at a small neighborhood bar may make $28,000 a year, while the manager of a large club can make an annual salary of more than $100,000. The cost of living coupled with how much time you want them to devote to your business will factor into how much they cost you. Many managers, especially general managers, will take a lower salary in exchange for a percentage of the sales. You and your accountant can discuss what kind of compensation package you can comfortably offer your managers.

Your front-of-the-house payroll is easy. Bartenders, servers, barbacks, and bussers all receive tips along with an hourly salary. Hosts are also often tipped out in a pre-arranged fashion—either a set amount each shift from each server/bartender or a percentage taken by the bookkeeper. Most of the staff will receive minimum wage. Sometimes more experienced bartenders and bar managers, who also work behind the bar for tips, receive a higher hourly salary. In some areas, bartenders receive a state minimum wage. In other areas, bartenders are unionized and must be paid accordingly.

> **Tip...**
>
> **Smart Tip**
> Contact your state labor commissioner's office to find out how much you have to pay your tipped employees hourly. Some states have a reduced minimum wage for servers and bartenders.

Drafting Your Team

Now that you know what positions you need to fill, it's time to sharpen your expectations and your observational skills. When hiring, you want to match the personality of the person you'rre hiring with that of the staff as a whole and with the kinds of people you are targeting as customers. Of course, above all, the candidate must be able to fulfill the job requirements.

Job Descriptions

Before you begin the hiring process, you should have written job descriptions for every position. Keep a laminated copy of each job description to show candidates during a job interview. They may realize right away that the job isn't for them. It's best to find these things out before either of you wastes time. If you'll expect certain employees to work on holidays, you need to specify that in the job description.

The Application

The first step in the hiring process is the application. Many bars use generic applications that ask for basic information. These types of applications are fine for bussers, prep cooks, dishwashers, barbacks, and hosts. However, if you're looking for professional servers, bartenders, line cooks, and especially managers, you'll find they have resume packets. Their resumes will provide more information than a generic application form, plus they often provide letters of recommendation. Still, you need to get all applicants to completely fill out an application, whether or not you're making them repeat information. The candidate's signature verifying the truth of the information on the application protects the owner in cases of deceit.

The Interview

Before you begin the interview process, you should develop a procedure. Perhaps you'll have initial interviews conducted by an assistant manager and final interviews conducted by you or the general manager. Perhaps you'll have an interview by committee. Some managers will have a candidate pretend to serve them to test their customer service skills.

Attempt to make the interview as comfortable as possible for the applicants. You want as close to the "real person" to come across as possible. Offer them something to drink, talk to them at a private table, and don't take phone calls or visitors during the interview. Give them your full attention, and you should be able to assess whether they'll fit in or not.

Now Hiring

Finding qualified applicants to staff your bar is like fishing. You can find a spot with hundreds of fish, but they're too small to keep. Or you can look for a spot to hook the big one, find it, catch it, and then never find anything there again. So the more spots you have to choose from, the better you'll do.

Most of the resources for gathering potential employees are free, but some can cost you. In his book *Running a Successful Bar* (BobTheBarGuy.com), Bob Johnson suggests some great ways to generate employee candidates, such as:

- *Current employees.* Use the resources you already have to generate referrals. Generally, your staff won't recommend someone unless they know their referral would do a good job.
- *Colleges.* Colleges and universities often have job boards where you can post a flier or listing. If the institution offers a hospitality degree, talk to the head of the department about potential candidates.
- *State employment offices.* These departments will often send you candidates that require training, but sometimes you'll find people with experience, too. They're a great resource, especially for entry-level jobs.
- *Bartending schools.* Many trade schools offer their graduates a placement service. These students have made an investment in this industry, so they're a great resource.
- *Signage.* You can get the attention of candidates in your community by hanging a temporary sign that says "NOW HIRING" outside your bar.
- *Be on the lookout.* If you see a server or bartender at another establishment who would be a great fit for your bar, you can tell them how impressed you are by their ability. Simply leave your card with them just in case they're thinking of moving on.

It may be easier for you to compare candidates if you ask them the same questions. Asking them all the same questions will also make it easier for you to compare and contrast candidates after they leave your office. But generally, the questions you choose to ask will be dictated by the tone of the conversation and the candidate's answers to the earlier questions. You should have a list of 20 or so questions from which to choose. Rarely will you ever ask that many, but your question list can serve as a reminder of all the different types of things you're looking for in an employee.

▲

⚠ Beware!

Be upfront about the shifts you have available to applicants in the interview. Sometimes managers give false hope about the income potential for servers and bartenders. If you do this, you risk losing a valuable employee, as well as the money it cost to train them.

Talk to candidates about your concept and what you want them to do to help bring it to life. Try to gauge their nonverbal reactions to what you say. Make sure they exhibit signs of great customer service (knowledgeable, good communicators). This will go a long way to discovering how they'll interact with your customers in casual conversation.

Interview questions can be as common as: "What was your least favorite part of your last job?" or as unique as "What would be your ideal uniform?" What you talk about isn't nearly as important as how the applicant speaks and listens. You'll be looking for different characteristics based on what you expect from the position. On page 119, you'll find a list of questions to ask bartending candidates. This will give you some ideas on the types of questions you would ask any potential employee. If you're specific with the description of the job, then creating interview questions for that position will flow easily.

Remember, though, that there are some questions that you can't ask during a job interview. Any questions that could be considered discriminatory, such as those about age, gender, nationality, religion, and marital or family status, are off limits.

Testing

Your interview process will give you an idea of what kind of personality a potential candidate has and how they will fit in with your staff and clientele. But when you're interviewing a bartender, you can't tell how well they make drinks. To test their mettle, you can give bartender candidates a written test concerning their knowledge of different liquors, drink recipes, and other aspects of the job. The best time for such a test (no more than a one-page test should be necessary) is upon their arrival for the first interview—after their application and resume have passed inspection. Kitchen managers often test line-cook applicants, too, to ensure they have the prerequisite knowledge for the position. A similar test can help you weed out server applicants who stretch, pad or simply fabricate their resumes. On pages 121

Bright Idea

Prospective employees, especially experienced ones, will come calling during slow business hours—usually between 3 and 5 P.M. The person you have on the floor or at the door during this time should know exactly how to greet and instruct the potential superstar team player. Make it part of their training to treat potential co-workers with respect.

Interview Questions for Bartenders

1. How long have you been working as a bartender?
2. What have you liked about your current (or last) job?
3. What have you disliked about your current (or last) job?
4. Was it your favorite bartending job so far? If not, what was and why?
5. In all your experience, which was your busiest job? Highest average sales intake?
6. In that job, what were your average sales?
7. What did you sell the most of—beer, wine, mixed drinks, or blended drinks?
8. How many kegs would you go through on a busy night? Who would change them?
9. Have you ever worked with or trained a barback?
10. What was your relationship with the cocktail servers? Did you oversee them during the shift? Did you make their schedules?
11. What was the most challenging part of your favorite job?
12. Have you had garnish responsibilities? Cutting, storing, and/or preparing?
13. How do you handle obscene, rude, or drunken behaviors from your guests?
14. In your favorite job, did you free-pour or measure? What was the measurement?
15. Did you work with pour-cost percentages? Each shift or each inventory check?
16. Did you handle inventory?
17. We have a _____ cash register system. Are you familiar with it? If not, what types and brands have you used?
18. What, if any, troubles have you had with co-workers wanting alcohol in inappropriate ways, such as a drink while on shift or a free drink for a visiting friend? How did you handle it? How would you handle it in the future?
19. Do you have any regular activities that may cause scheduling conflicts? Do you prefer working days or nights? How about swing shifts?
20. How far do you live from here?
21. Will you be able to get to work by the scheduled start time?
22. What else do you do besides work? What are your dreams and ambitions?
23. Are you a regular customer at a bar? Do you ever get free drinks from that bar? (A truthful answer to this question should in no way cause you to mistrust the candidate.)
24. What would be your ideal uniform?
25. What do you think you would bring to our bar's concept?

and 122, you'll find tests you can use for bartenders and servers. Tests to examine your prospective cooks will vary depending on your menu.

You may decide to interview the candidate before giving them the test or vice versa. It all depends what works best for you and your managers. If you give the test first, going over the test as the interview begins can be a good way to start.

Rules of the Game

Now that you've found a great set of recruits, let's open those doors! Your staff should be raring to go. They should ooze energy and stand on years of great experience in the industry. They should eagerly await the opportunities to spread the image and themes you've conceptualized.

Every member of your staff should show up on time when training is about to start. That's right—you have to train them even if they know the bar business better than you do. There are as many different ways to do things in a bar as there are bars. For every decision you make, there are half a dozen other ways to do the same thing.

Can They Cope?

Hiring and training new employees is very expensive. It costs an estimated $300 per trainee. It is also an exhausting endeavor, both for the people doing the hiring and those who train. Therefore, the interviewer should continually ask themselves if the applicant can cope with the duties of the job. To COPE, they will need to have the following:

- ○ *Certainty.* Is the person confident they have the knowledge this position requires?
- ○ *Occupational aptitude.* Do they possess the skills and experience needed?
- ○ *Physically fit.* Are they in proper shape for the physical demands of the job? Servers often have to do a lot of walking around the bar. Bartenders and barbacks often have to do heavy lifting of ice and beer kegs. Your applicants should be aware of this aspect of the job, and they should be up to the challenge.
- ○ *Emotionally capable.* Do they have the right personality and mind-set for the position?

Pre-Employment Test for Bartenders

Name: _____   Date: _____

1. What type of liquor is Maker's Mark?

   _____

2. What type of glass would you use to serve Hennesy V.S.O.P.?

   _____

   What does V.S.O.P. stand for?

   _____

3. Circle the one true phrase of the following:

   a) All whiskeys and scotches are bourbons.
   b) All scotches and bourbons are whiskeys.
   c) All bourbons and whiskeys are scotches.

4. Describe the following drink instructions:

   Double _____   Tall _____
   Splash _____   Dry _____
   Extra dry _____   Float _____
   Rocks _____   Frozen _____

5. How many ounces make up a liter? _____

   How many ounces are in a 750-ml bottle? _____

   If you pour 1½-oz. shots, how many shots are in a liter bottle? _____

6. If IDs are checked at the door, you don't have to worry about serving minors.

   ❑ True ❑ False

7. What do you look for to see if an ID is fake?

   _____

   _____

8. What distilled spirit has the nickname "cactus whiskey"? _____

9. What does "top shelf" mean? _____

   Give three "top shelf" examples:

   1. _____
   2. _____
   3. _____

10. What is your favorite drink to make?

    _____

▲

Pre-Employment Test for Servers

Name: _____   Date: _____

1. If your guest asks for a martini, what alcohol do you think they want?

_____

2. What garnish(es) would you apply to the following drinks?
   Martini: _____ or _____
   Gibson: _____ Gimlet: _____
   Whiskey sour: _____ Tom Collins: _____
   Margarita: _____ Mai Tai: _____
   Cubra Libra: _____ Jack Daniels and Coke: _____

3. How old is a person born on July 14, 1979? _____

4. Total the following prices:

A) $14.50	B) $12.75	C) $10.00	D) $18.25
3.50	9.00	2.50	1.50
11.25	5.50	11.50	7.00
	18.25		10.00
			2.75

5. What is 15 percent of:
   A) $40 _____ B) $36.60 _____ C) $9 _____

6. Give an example of what would constitute an inappropriate action toward you by a customer:_____

_____

What would you do about such an action?

_____

_____

7. On a scale from 1 to 10 (1 being least important), how would you rate the importance of liking the bartender(s) you work with?_____

8. Define the following:
   Up _____ On the rocks_____
   Tall _____ Flag _____
   Virgin _____ Dry_____
   Extra dry_____

9. What usually covers the rim of a margarita glass?_____

10. What mixed drink would you say you've served the most?_____

Therefore, you need to have a point of reference. In your case, it should be the employee handbook.

In your bar, you write the rules—even if you're taking over an existing operation. You don't want to jump in and make lots of grand, sweeping changes at once, but you do want to make sure you clearly communicate what you expect from your staff.

You can start by holding an all-staff meeting to introduce yourself. At that time, if you know how you want the behaviors of the staff to change, and you have a new employee handbook ready, then you could act as if you're starting from scratch. Be careful, though. Many new owners end up alienating their staffs, and consequently their customers, by moving too far too fast with policy changes, dress code changes, price increases, and so on.

If you're opening a new bar or coming into an established bar, closing it and reopening it with a different name, then you'll need to have your employee manual ready to go before training starts. This manual should act as an extension of you and your management team. You should follow the rules set forth just as reverently as you expect your staff to follow them.

Writing the Playbook

All your employees should be well aware of what's expected of them and what will happen if they break the rules. Your employees will feel a true sense of team spirit if they're all held to the same standards.

Unfortunately, a large percentage of employees "never get around" to reading the handbook. The only way you can hope to combat this is to make the rules as short and simple as possible. You should also ask them to sign a document stating that they have read and understand the manual. Keep this form in their personnel files to protect yourself legally. Remember, your whole team will have to live by these rules, including you and your managers. You'll need to create policies for some or all of the following issues:

- *Dress code.* You should describe the appearance you want from each position. Be specific. Will you supply part or all of the uniforms for your employees? Will you buy the uniforms for them and then deduct the cost from their paychecks? Will you take a deposit from their pay for certain items, like aprons? Some bars seem to have no dress code—every time you go in, the servers and bartenders are dressed comfortably in jeans or shorts and T-shirts. However, even they have rules. You won't see foul or offensive language on their apparel. You won't see the uniform of another food/beverage place on your server or bartender. However, you may see a T-shirt advertising a brand of liquor or beer.

- *Off-limits areas*. Are employees allowed in the office? If not, where do they do their cash-outs? If someone is waiting for an employee to get off work, where should they wait? Who's allowed behind the bar? Who's allowed behind the line? When and for how long?

- *Behaviors*. What actions, physical and verbal, are unacceptable? You must define sexual harassment and other unacceptable behaviors in terms that are easy to understand. Make sure the policies you

> **Smart Tip** *Tip...*
>
> Your employee handbook should contain your mission statement, the job descriptions of all the positions employed, your employees' potential benefits and other rewards, and succinct policy descriptions of things like theft and sexual harassment.

set forth on this subject are clear and consistently enforced.

How should an employee who has been harassed report the incident? What steps will be taken to follow up on the report?

- *Crime and punishment*. Who will you discipline? For what? And how? What actions or behaviors would call for immediate termination? Theft? Not showing up for a shift without calling? Who's responsible for the discipline of whom? How do federal, state, and/or local regulations affect disciplining your staff? For example, where, by law, are your employees allowed to have nonalcoholic drinks while on shift? Don't be surprised if this section of your rules changes constantly. You'll learn as you go along which offenses you can or can't tolerate from your staff and which cause very few problems.

- *Staff evaluations*. When and how often will employees be evaluated? Who will conduct the evaluations? This section should also cover probationary periods, raises, and promotions.

- *Meals and breaks*. Which of your employees are allowed to eat during a shift and which are not? What are the regulations in your area concerning meal breaks? In some states, a five-hour shift constitutes a half-hour break. If you go with one bartender, who will fill in for them when they need a break? Or will you schedule shorter shifts? Will you feed your cooks and dishwashers for free? Will you offer employee discounts on food?

- *Staff as guests*. Are your employees allowed to hang out in the bar after work? Do they get a complimentary beer or other alcoholic beverage when they're finished working? (Is that legal where you are?) Do they have to change out of their uniforms to sit in the bar as a guest? If employees visit your bar on their days off, do they receive a discount? How much?

- *Smoking*. Are your employees allowed to smoke at all during working hours? If so, when, where, and under what circumstances? What are the laws in your area concerning smoking?

- *Handling money.* Are your employees who handle cash—servers, bartenders, and cashiers—responsible for all the money they ring up? What if they take a bad check? What procedures must they follow to accept a check? What if the guest just leaves the check on the table without talking to the server or bartender? What if a customer leaves without paying the bill (dine and dash)?

- *Mistakes.* Will you make bartenders pay for drink mistakes? Will the servers have to pay for incorrectly ordered items? Some managers make employees pay for mistakes after they've made a few and the causes have been figured out. However, other managers warn against this policy because it may cause a high turnover rate for your staff. After all, to err is human.

Beware!

Many people in this industry smoke cigarettes. In your employee manual, be careful about using phrases like "You can only smoke on your break." Many employees won't be able to take a prescribed break at a pre-set time. Usually, they take breaks during lulls in business. You want to prevent smokers in need of a cigarette from giving bad service.

- *Tips.* Who claims what portion of their tips as income, and how do they go about claiming them for tax purposes? There are computer systems available that will ask your servers to claim their tips when they clock out. Most servers and bartenders typically claim about 8 to 10 percent of total sales as their take-home amount for tips.. Still, the IRS requires that all tips are claimed, so you should make sure your employees are aware of the law.

Your most heavily tipped employees—bartenders and servers—will almost certainly need to tip out some of your other employees, such as bussers, barbacks, expediters, and hosts. You need to decide how you'll monitor these tip-outs. The industry standard dictates that 2.25 percent of each bartender's sales should go to the barback. Likewise, 2.25 percent of each server's total sales should go to the bussers. If you have more than one barback or busser on the floor at a time, they should be tipped out based on your scheduling and tip-out policy. For example, if you have two bussers who are jointly responsible for table maintenance and assisting all the servers, then they should split the total tip-out take evenly. If, on the other hand, a busser is assigned to a server or a section, then they should be tipped out individually by the servers they assist.

The rule of thumb for hostesses and expediters is first to decide whether or not they get tipped at all. Secondly, you should create a standard tip-out per shift—like $2 per shift to each host and from each server and bartender. How and what your servers tip out to your bartenders depends on how your operation is structured. If your bartender acts like a busser for the server by clearing tables and fetching condiments, then the bartender should receive a higher percentage. If the bartender only makes the drinks, then they should receive a fixed percentage of sales from each server on the shift.

- *Trainers and trainees.* If you're located in a state that allows you to pay tipped employees less than minimum wage, you must pay those employees at least minimum wage while they're training if they don't get to keep the tips they earn. How many trainers will you have at one time? Will you pay them a higher hourly wage when they train? Will you increase their

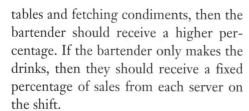

Dollar Stretcher

Be on the lookout for employees who want more work. Instead of hiring a seasonal employee, you might give a host or two some extra shifts to check hats and coats in the winter. Try having a busser help out as a barback on a busy night. Cross-training will save you time and money in the long run.

regular pay, whether or not they're training? Will you feed them for free? Will they get the free food only when they train or every shift? How does an employee become a trainer?

- *Scheduling and payday.* When and how often will you issue paychecks to your staff? When will schedules be posted? Will you promise regular schedules to any members of your staff? Which employees? What happens to an employee who is one minute late for a shift? Five minutes late?

- *Sickness.* Whose responsibility is it to cover shifts for sick employees? How far in advance must a sick person call to inform the manager?

- *Hygiene.* What are your expectations of your employees' cleanliness? Will you demand frequent hand washing? What kind and how much jewelry is appropriate? Do you expect freshly pressed uniforms? Do you have any regulations for facial hair? Generally, men and women with long hair should have it tied back when serving food and beverages.

- *Internal conflicts.* How should your employees go about airing grievances? Have you given them outlets for complaints they may have about your policies, their supervisor, and their co-workers? Should they attempt to work out

Beware!

R.C. Colvin, Round Table Bar & Grill owner in Niles, Michigan, took over an existing operation. He learned the importance of product control very quickly. "I had a couple of people working for me, really good, hard-working employees, who would lose, give away, or accidentally not ring up two or three cases of beer a night on a Thursday or Friday. We tightened that up in a real big hurry."

squabbles on their own, or do you want them to go to their supervisor/manager?

- *Safety and security.* You owe it to yourself and to your business to make sure your staff understands what to do in any type of emergency situation. You also should make sure to educate your employees about safety precautions and preventable hazards, such as hurting their backs by lifting incorrectly or what to do when a glass breaks in the ice bin.

Training Camp

Training your employees boils down to orienting them with both the employee manual and their job descriptions. They need to know the things they're supposed to do and the way they're supposed to do them. The first time they see the inner workings of your bar, they'll be with the trainer. If your trainer is a good one, he or she will watch everything the new person does, like a third-base coach watches his player swing the bat in baseball.

Generally, you'll choose one of your veteran employees to train new hires—one whose instincts, knowledge, and behaviors you trust. The first day of training usually consists of following the trainer around as he or she performs the job. A lot of information gets thrown at new employees right off the bat. Expect and encourage your new employees to ask questions.

Basic Training

You'll want to draft a training schedule, but prepare to be flexible. For example, if a server walks in with 10 years of experience in the business and has worked with your computer system at another bar for five years, chances are good he won't need the full eight shifts of training you prescribe to new servers. Get your servers and bartenders out serving customers as soon as your trainer says they're ready. Not everyone learns at the same speed.

Your rules, policies, and expectations should all be laid out simply during training. Your trainer will supervise as the new employee takes over more and more of the duties required of the position. Again, a lot of

Bright Idea

Draft your employee manual and training manual on a computer so you can change the documents easily. Label the first page with the date and version number. Keep a hard copy of previous versions so you can reference what was changed over time. Your employee handbook can act as a living communication device for your whole team.

information will confront a trainee all at once. Your trainer must be patient and respectful.

You and your managers will hire people you think will do a good job and fit into your team. Unfortunately, no one is perfect. A dud or two will get through your radar, even if you hone it to needle-point perfection. Ideally, your training system will weed out these duds. So you need trainers who can not only teach but inspect. They should do everything they can, without prejudice, to help a new person perform the duties required. Yet they should truthfully declare the abilities or inabilities of a new employee.

To determine the readiness of new employees, you can test them on the information needed to fulfill their job descriptions. Let them know the scope of the test and when they will need to take it. Determine beforehand what percentage of accuracy is needed to allow a trainee on the floor. Also, decide ahead of time if and when they can retake the test if they don't pass.

Set for Success

After your employees have completed their training, you want to make sure you do everything you can to make them successful. One of the best ways to do this is to remain in constant communication with them.

Here are some of the communications you should post for your staff:

- *Schedules*. In addition to regular shift schedules, any daily, weekly, or monthly chores should have corresponding work schedules with space for dates of cleanings and initials of the person who completed the work. All schedules should be posted at least five days before the scheduled week begins. Shift-change forms, if you use them, should hang near the schedule. Employees can use these forms to switch shifts or cover shifts for each other. They should always be signed by a manager.

- *Job responsibilities*. As specifically as you can, you should make out charts containing the different positions you employ and a list of duties for each.

- *Maps*. Your employees should have access to a map of the bar's setup, complete with table numbers, at all times. You may

Bright Idea

If you go to the trouble of updating charts and job descriptions for your employees to see, they should at least read them. To encourage this, you may consider slipping in a line like "The first two employees per shift who tell me they read this get a free meal." Make sure you date all the fliers you post.

rearrange tables or entertainment setups depending on what type of activities or promotions are happening. Communicate these changes to your staff well in advance of the shift.

Flagrant Fouls

Every team has ups and downs on its way through the season. Sometimes, the downs are caused by upsetting and intolerable behaviors on the parts of the team members. In this business, theft and employee turnover create major problems for employers.

Theft

The rate at which bartenders steal money has alarmed and aggravated bar management consultant Bob Johnson so much that he had to stop going into bars undercover to look for theft. "We estimate that 70 to 80 percent of bartenders steal," says Johnson. "Theft is created by owners and managers who don't put controls in place so they won't steal. Because owners don't know how to do that, they actually force their bartenders to steal over a period of time. I did surveillance for five years, and it was disgusting. Some of these people would steal right in front of everybody, and nobody was saying anything."

Bartenders and servers have the most opportunities to steal from your business, but you also have to watch out in the back of the house. Always make sure someone there is held responsible for ensuring you're not "losing" any product. For more information on how to prevent and detect theft in your business, read Chapters 9 and 13.

Turnover

As mentioned earlier in this chapter, the cost of hiring and training new employees runs high. You not only pay more in labor while you train a new person, but for a while after, as your new servers continue to learn. They'll have to figure out what product they want to recommend, the fastest meals available, and many other things that take getting used to. There's a learning curve in the business of bartending, serving, cooking, and managing. Whether or not they've had experience, these professionals have to learn new procedures and some new products for every job they accept. Until they find their niche within your team of employees, they may not bring in the sales you both want. Because of this, a high turnover rate can crush your business.

Turnover rates soar high in the bar industry, especially in the front of the house, where incomes can be inconsistent and attitudes can spoil quickly. To help combat this, start with the application and interview. Ron Newman, the sports bar owner in

Manhattan Beach, California, offers this advice: "When it comes to turnover, one of the things we do is look at how much time they have left at school if they're students. That lets you know if they're going to be around for a couple years. In our operation, most of our people are pretty young—I'd say 21 to 30—and we look for people who don't change jobs a whole lot."

On the other hand, you can find veterans of the business, who jump from place to place, that could make great additions to your staff. They may work in certain areas for the ski season or other hobby, then return when it is over. This type of journeyman will usually give plenty of notice if they're upfront about their lifestyles. Then they can come back and work for you later with little or no training.

> **Bright Idea**
> Check with your local community college for inexpensive classes on managing small businesses. You may send your managers to these classes to improve their abilities, or even take one or two yourself. They often provide tips on conflict resolution and hiring, training, managing, and retaining personnel.

What Have You Learned?

In this chapter, you've learned the impact your employees can have on the success of your business, and the impact you can have on your employees. Always have your bar fully stocked and ready to go, and have your employees ready and in place.

In the next chapter, we're going to get into a great deal of fun . . . your entertainment options. You can decide what you're going to do to entertain your guests, and what kind of people and facilities you'll need to provide the entertainment.

Let Us
Entertain You

A primary function of bar-related businesses is to engage customers. So the secret is figuring out how to constantly give your guests the entertainment options that keep them coming back to your bar.

What you do and how much you spend on entertainment depends on your target customers. If you're opening a nightclub, then you'd better aim at perfecting the music and dance scene in your bar. If you're a neighborhood tavern, perhaps a jukebox and a pool table will suffice. Things to consider when deciding the "diversions" you offer include what your target groups want and where they get it now.

For example, if you want your customer pool to brim with energetic twentysomethings, and you want to keep them occupied with pool tables, dartboards, and video games, then you'd better find out where they go to play now. If the hot spot to play pool and drink beer is a block away from your building, then you're throwing your line into a highly competitive fishing hole—prepare yourself properly. However, if your competitor clearly targets an older clientele with a higher income and is located in the next town, then you are more likely to attract the volume of guests necessary for success.

Finger to the Wind

Because you have carefully decided what types of customers your operation can successfully convert into returning guests, you have a major head start on what entertainment options you will need to supply.

It's imperative that you establish a plan to attract returning guests, and keep an eye locked on that plan. For example, The Fifth, the Miami nightclub managed by Gerry Kelly, offers a variety of outlandish entertainment, everything from fire eaters to opera singers. You don't have to go that far to provide a variety to your guests:

Many clubs showcase different kinds of music on different nights. But if your muddy sound system disturbs your patrons instead of encouraging them with crisp, clean tones or your lighting scheme sends them running off with headaches, then it won't matter what kind of music you've invested in.

Likewise, if you're planning to open a sports bar, you must consider your layout if you plan to have equipment such as ping-pong, foosball, or pool tables. Is there enough room? Can you put video games in high-traffic areas without having customers trip over them? Will the machines and tables make your bar seem cluttered instead of inviting? What rules will you have to establish and how will you enforce them?

Beware!
Don't assume that the entertainment you like (or can afford) will also please your customers. Before settling on the type of entertainment you're going to offer, ask the following questions: Do you have the capacity to accommodate your entertainment choice? What entertainment options do your competitors offer? And most important, what are your customers asking for?

Diversions of Choice

How you choose to entertain your customers depends on who they are and how you perceive what they want. You will also have to consider your physical space and financial budget when deciding on entertainment. The following breakdown gives you an overview of options for delivering amusement to your patrons.

Performance-Based Entertainment

- ○ Solo musicians or bands
- ○ Small acoustic groups
- ○ Comedians
- ○ Improv groups
- ○ Big-name music acts
- ○ Magicians
- ○ Dancing
- ○ DJ/VJ crowd handling
- ○ Special effects
- ○ Lighting shows
- ○ Interactive trivia games

Nonperformance-Based Entertainment

- ○ Televised sports
- ○ Video games
- ○ Pool tables
- ○ Air hockey tables
- ○ Dartboards
- ○ Foosball tables
- ○ Ping-pong tables
- ○ Jukeboxes
- ○ Pre-recorded music

The entertainment options you have to choose from fall into two camps: performance-based and nonperformance-based. The former would include live performances, dancing, and interactive trivia games, whereas pool tables, jukeboxes, and television sets fall into the latter group of activities.

Nonperformance-Based Entertainment

Following is the most common types of nonperformance-based entertainment.

Television

Long, long ago, in a time before DVDs and pocket televisions, people gathered in bars to watch TV—the black-and-white sets. (Remember those?) Now we average more than two TV sets per home, and many of them are in high definition. Yet people still congregate in bars to watch certain events on TV. Sports of every imaginable kind bring throngs of celebrating customers to bars. If this is the kind of bar you want to have, then you'll probably want to obtain more than just basic cable for your TVs.

There are as many different deals on programming packages (e.g., the NFL package) as there are satellites in the sky.

High-definition, flat-screen TVs are becoming more popular (and cheaper!), and you can get service from satellite TV providers or cable companies. Be careful and be patient when looking to hook yourself up. You have seemingly endless options when it comes to how you use TVs in your bar. You could build a wall of TVs, each broadcasting a different sporting event. You could just have one set, in a political-themed bar, beaming C-SPAN and CNN to your customers.

Dollar Stretcher

If you plan to have TVs in your bar, you'll want to have either a satellite system or cable. Unless your bar is small, you should have more than one TV so lots of customers can view them (especially in a sports bar). Talk to your cable company. It will often negotiate a deal for lower rates when you have multiple TVs.

How much you'll have to pay to use TVs in this manner depends on where you live and the kind of deals you can strike. More and more cable companies are offering combination packages that include TV and phone service, as well as internet access. You may be able to save by signing up to have all these services delivered by one company. Since the costs vary so much depending on your location, contact your local cable and satellite providers to find out how much it will cost to set up a system in your bar. For an example, see the "Cable TV Cost chart below.

Cable TV Cost—Public Viewing Package

First TV Set: $99.95 per month
Each Additional TV Set: $10.00 per month

These prices came from a Boston area cable company. The package includes regular cable and a "sports pack," with high-definition programming included.

Video Games and Pool Tables

Coin-operated machines—whether jukeboxes, pool tables, or video games—can generate quite a bit of income for your operation. You can easily find distributors of "Amusement Devices" online or in the Yellow Pages, or by asking other users like bowling alleys, restaurants, pool halls, etc. Video games often malfunction or wear out, so you need to pay special attention to the service available for the video games you purchase or lease. By asking other owners/managers about their games, you'll learn a lot about the reputations of their distributors. You can also ask the distributors for a list of references you may contact.

When renting video games, you may be required to share the revenue with the distributor. Typically, you can expect to keep 50 percent of the take. You may be end up making an agreement for a lower percentage, say 40 percent, to ensure better, more popular games, though. Remember, no matter what your percentage is, the more the game is used, the more you make.

Beware!
The lure of fast money has turned many a human into a gambler. Today, the rules on gambling, and what constitutes a casino, change quickly. Video poker and other payoff games are legal in some places in the United States. Keep in mind that the government always wants it's cut, especially when it comes to gambling money.

Where you find pool tables, you find rules. Be sure to clearly post your rules somewhere near your pool tables and include policies for who plays when. You can use a chalkboard to list those waiting to play the winner of an ongoing game. Another option is to have the players lay their money for the next game on the table.

Contests such as pool tournaments, dart tournaments, and video game tournaments can really spice up your slower nights. You could charge a small fee to enter the tournament, then donate a portion of the proceeds to charity. Your bar's overall profit would increase because more people will be in your bar drinking and eating.

Your customers' interests will dictate what kind of tournaments you sponsor. If the interest is there, and you hold regular tournaments—every other week or every month— you will see an increase in participation, hence an increase in your bar's business.

Darts get broken and lost. Pool table felt wears thin and needs replacing. Video games grow tired and sometimes malfunction or break. Ask yourself who pays when these things happen. If you do, then you may want to keep the income from your game separate in your bookkeeping so you can pay the expenses out of that account. This will also help you to determine whether your games are profitable.

Jukeboxes and Background Music

Jukeboxes offer interaction between your customers and their environment. People can get excited about choosing their own music, but other patrons may not always agree with their taste. If you have the baseball game blaring from a radio or TV, and you don't cover or unplug the jukebox, don't be surprised if an angry patron complains about not being able to hear the songs they picked and paid for. There's nothing wrong with blaring the game if it's what the crowd wants. Just make sure you eliminate the jukebox option during that time.

Performance-Based Entertainment

Following the most common types of performance-based entertainment.

Live Performances

Live performances—from solo pianists to comedians to rock bands—are what many people think of as "entertainment" at a bar. Booking these performers can be tricky, or it can be simple. Depending on your concept and desired atmosphere, you can either book complete unknowns, who impress you with their acts, or the locally famous acts, who are most likely represented by a manager. You may also find yourself somewhere in between.

One way or another, you or your designated representative (manager, promoter, or booking agent) should audition or screen the performances you're considering. Nothing empties a room like an offensive stand-up comic or an off-key lead singer. Also, be mindful of what the performers will have to compete with for the attention of your patrons. Solo performers, magicians, and comedians may not want to compete against the ding-a-ding-ring of a pinball machine or sports fans cheering for a game on TV.

Do you want your club to be a venue for big-name acts? If your answer is "yes," choose carefully and plan accordingly. Make sure your local market will support the big-name band or performer you bring in to play for them. Find out which local radio stations cater to your target audience, and what kind of music they play. If you book a top-selling heavy metal band but your community is full of gospel music fans, you could be in some trouble. Also, keep in mind that you're going to be open for business on nights you don't have the big names coming in to perform.

"When you go into music, it can get very pricey," warns Bob Brenlin, the Seattle pub owner. "An issue most people don't realize is you have to pay BMI, ASCAP, etc., for live music. It can cost you a lot of money every year, and they just hound you for it." Using music as entertainment in your bar will almost always cost you something you didn't see coming. Read "Paying the Piper" on page 137 to shed some light on the hidden costs. Brenlin estimates that using live music costs at least $2,000 a year just in association fees.

The DJ/VJ

As you were reading about your bar's personnel in Chapter 10, you may have thought "What about a DJ? I can't run my nightclub without a DJ." That's true. Although not all bars need DJs, most nightclubs do. Your DJ may be an employee of your bar, or he may be someone who you hire on certain nights. Either way, you have

Paying the Piper

Many startup bar owners don't anticipate the cost of using music in their bar. If you play copyrighted music in your establishment, you'll need to pay royalties to the artists' associations.

However, there are two exceptions to this rule where you don't have to pay the royalties:

1. If you don't charge a cover fee of your customers, you won't have to pay royalties for coin-operated jukebox music. (You may need to register your jukebox with the artist association, though.)
2. If you use a "home quality" sound system (noncommercial equipment) in a small bar, then you're exempt from paying royalties.

If you play music in your operation and don't meet either of these exceptions, you have to pay royalties. Remember that musicians make part of their living through their royalties. Be thankful you can play the music in your bar, and pay the fees gladly.

There are three major performing rights associations:

1. *ASCAP (American Society of Composers, Authors, & Publishers).* 1 Lincoln Plaza, New York, NY 10023, (800) 95-ASCAP, ascap.com
2. *BMI (Broadcast Music Incorporated).* 320 W. 57th St., New York, NY 10019, (212) 586-2000, bmi.com
3. *SESAC (Society of European Stage Authors and Composers).* 55 Music Square E., Nashville, TN 37203 (headquarters), (800) 826-9996, sesac.com

To protect your bar from infringing on copyrights, contact each of the associations to obtain an application and find out more about music licenses.

to pay him. If your resources are limited, you may have to train them. If you can afford to hire a seasoned veteran, you have to know what you're looking for when you interview and hire them. The reason we didn't talk about DJs along with the rest of your personnel is because your DJ is more like a performer than a server or a bartender. The DJ's primary function is to encourage your guests to get out on the dance floor and have a great time. To do this effectively, they must be consistent without becoming boring, and they must always keep the pace moving. Your DJ is the life of the party!

In addition to playing music, many night-clubs mount television screens throughout their facilities and show music videos on them. Which videos to show and when to run them can affect the atmosphere of your bar, too. Some places strive to match slower songs with a corresponding music video. Your reason for showing videos should be just as calculated as everything else that you add to your bar's atmosphere. If you decide you want to have videos, you'll need someone to operate and manage the equipment throughout the night. In some smaller operations, your DJ can take over the job, but you'll most likely need to hire a video jockey or VJ. If your VJ talks to the crowd, too, then you must hold them to the same high standards you would your DJ.

> **Fun Fact**
>
> The term "payola" refers to the gifts and money showered on radio disc jockeys by record companies to promote specific songs. Payola bribes spread like wildfire through the 1950s due to the great influence of radio DJs on record sales. Your nightclub DJs may have some influence on music trends in your area, too!

When hiring a DJ/VJ, have candidates audition for you, just like a musician or comedian would. You should discuss payment requirements as well as their experience during the interview, but you should withhold judgment about their abilities until they come in and take over the booth for a shift. Some candidates won't even make it through a whole shift before you give them the proverbial hook. But if they do, you should pay them for their time, whether or not you decide to hire them. Write down a list of objectives you would like to see candidates achieve during their auditioning shifts. You could include several different promotions you want the DJ/VJ to promote to the crowd between songs, such as drink specials or upcoming events. Also, you may give candidates an idea of the tempo you want them to achieve and maintain.

Nightclubs that have dancing as their main focus usually charge a cover at the door. When your customers pay to get in your bar, and they're having fun dancing, they will take offense if they have to listen to a DJ/VJ rambling on and on about next week's show. Keep this in mind as you're looking for the right DJ or VJ. Your ideal DJ/VJ will not only do a great job, but will build a reputation and then a following.

Interactive Trivia Games

The last type of performance-based entertainment we're going to cover may throw you a curve. In the bar industry today, interactive trivia games—pitting your customers against each other and against other players all over the world—are still popular. One advantage to this type of entertainment is the supplemental source of income derived from selling advertising spots on the game monitors. If your customers get hooked on the game, you can bet they'll return. This type of game might also help provide a happy and exciting environment in your bar.

The disadvantages could follow along the same lines. You may have to pay a lot of money for the use of the equipment and for the subscriptions to satellite services. Another possible disadvantage tells why this type of game is performance-based while your run-of-the-mill video game is nonperformance-based. The intensely energetic mood created by this type of game may alienate your guests who don't want to play the game. They may end up saying "We could go to Joe's Neighborhood Bar, but they have that loud, obnoxious trivia game."

Lights! Camera! Sound!

If you're planning to open a nightclub, the dance scene in your club will be a significant factor in its success. The appeal and comfort of your dance floor, the selection and clarity of your sound system, and the synchronization and appropriateness of your lighting will all determine the fate of your nightclub. As we pointed out earlier, you could build the perfect dancing atmosphere in your club only to have potential patrons chased off by a boring DJ. Conversely, you could hire the best DJ in the world, and he might end up performing in an empty room if your sound system fluctuates or the dance floor is so small the dancers can't move.

Many bars, even small taverns, can set aside space in their facility for performances. "Open mike" nights and karaoke are just two examples of how you can liven things up in any bar with performances/activities. When these are the kind of entertainment options you want to provide, you don't necessarily need large-scale or top-quality lighting and sound systems. If these activities are supplemental diversions for your customers, not the focus of your mission as a bar, then your money could do more for your operation if it were invested in areas other than lighting and sound.

Beware!

Lighting, sound, and other technical experts are often salespeople. If they elevate the value of the equipment or service, they make money for their store or for themselves. To make sure you're getting the best deal possible, get at least two professional opinions before you make any buying decisions.

Now that we've covered the types of entertainment options you have, let's look at some of the dos and don'ts involved in designing and equipping your bar for live entertainment or a dance club.

Dancing the Night Away

If your nightclub is open during the day, oxymoron and all, you may want to set tables and chairs on your dance floor to serve drinks and lunch. This may sound strange since it usually happens the other way around. Many bars clear out tables and chairs to make room for people to dance. If you plan to put tables and chairs on the dance floor, be careful not to scratch or damage the floor, and make sure you clean it before the night shift comes in.

The size of your dance floor depends on your capacity and how many people you want to have out there dancing. (Remember: The more people dance, the thirstier they become!) How big a stage area you need depends on the types of acts you want to bring into your bar. If you plan to build a stage in your facility, try to predict how it will affect the flow of your staff and guests every minute you're open, not just when the show is on.

Sound Choices

Your decisions in this area all depend on your priorities for your bar. Look back at your mission statement. If you want your nightclub to set trends for the dance world, then you'll need to work with professional sound system consultants and invest in high-priced equipment.

On the other hand, if you just want a casual place for people to have fun together, you should still have a conversation with a consultant or sound engineer, but you might choose a sound system in the midprice range.

Hey, You! What Are You Looking At?

A television set picks up signals from the outside via antennas and tuners, whereas video screens or monitors get signals directly from a player or a camera. In a dance club, screens typically are scattered throughout the room so everyone can see the pictures.

You may need to pay licensing fees to show videos and the like in your bar. Just as you have to pay to rebroadcast music or perform it, the companies that produce videos have copyrights and groups protecting them. If you enter into any deal with a video program supplier, make sure you know who's responsible for paying the applicable licensing fees. Bring your lawyer into the deal if you have any doubts

Smile, You're On . . .

Your reason for having a dance scene in your bar in the first place is so your customers can have fun. Many clubs hire people to walk around the club with a movie camera to film the people and events of the evening. They either put the footage up on the screen as they're taping or play it back later in the evening. Cameras are also used to make it easier for all your guests to watch dance floor activities like limbo contests or to identify dance contest finalists among the crowd of participants. Depending on the privacy laws in your jurisdiction, you may or may not need to get permission from your patrons before they're videotaped. Again, this is where you should involve your lawyer to be absolutely sure. As you visualize your operation, keep your attorney informed about all your plans, just in case you may be affected or hindered by the laws.

Everything Looks Great!

How you light your bar's stage and/or dance floor will depend on what type of entertainment you plan to offer. If you showcase a succession of solo musicians, you'll only need a spotlight aimed at them. If you want to draw customers with a light show, then you'll obviously have to invest in a more complex lighting system to succeed. Which system you should choose and how much you'll have to spend depends on where you are, what you want, and who is selling it to you. Laser light shows, in addition to multicolored dance lights, are standards on the dance club scene. Sparkling, glittering balls may also hover, spinning above the sweating dancers and playing tricks with the lights.

Special effects, just like lighting tricks, have come a long way, yet some stay the same. You'll still see fog machines, neon colors, and confetti blowers in the toolbox of your effects designer. If your venue showcases big-name bands, they may bring their own special effects show and technicians to make it all happen. If you're among the smaller venues giving chances to new bands, you and your lighting person may have opportunities to experiment with special effects in conjunction with the band.

To choose the entertainment options your bar will supply, it's important to revisit your mission statement and your overall concept. Do you have the customers you want? If so, what do they want to do, see, and hear when they come to your bar? If not, what do you need to do differently to attract your desired clientele? Or should you adjust to meet the desires of the customers you have?

You have seen how many different choices you'll have to make. Many times you won't have to go anywhere to get the information you need to make your entertainment decisions. Salesmen of all kinds will try to tell you what your bar needs to compete. When it comes to equipping your bar with lighting and sound systems, acquire as much knowledge as you can about the deal you're offered and what you'll get for your money.

With all your equipment, personnel, and entertainment in place, it's time to get ready to open those doors. Now all you have to do is fill your bar with customers who will enjoy what you've created. In Chapter 12, you'll discover how to plan and execute promotions—and learn other ways to fill your bar to capacity on a regular basis.

Creating the
Buzz for Your Biz:
Marketing

Now that you have your entertainment in place and ready to go, it's time to start planning how you're going to get people into your bar to enjoy it. Just like any other aspect of operating your bar, marketing is an ongoing process. Many bar owners think marketing is the most fun and exciting aspect of running a bar. The entrepreneurs we interviewed agreed that traditional advertising, whether in newspapers, magazines, on TV or on the radio, didn't bring as much reward for the cost as it does for many other types of businesses. Generating a buzz for your bar will mostly come from word-of-mouth and the special promotions you set up.

"The only cost-effective way to advertise a bar is word-of-mouth," says bar management consultant Bob Johnson of Clearwater, South Carolina. "When you don't have word-of-mouth working for you, you're in serious trouble. It's not necessarily terminal. There are still ways to get some advertising and marketing out there without spending a ton of money. But anytime you reach into your own pocket to buy advertising for a bar, it's not good."

Dollar Stretcher

If you plan your grand opening with enough notice and really make it unusual and exciting, you can save money on advertising by marketing to your local media. A new bar in town is news, and a newspaper article or a segment on the television news can get a lot more attention than a paid advertisement.

Don't Go It Alone

A vital ingredient of successful marketing and promotion in a bar is to have one point person. Someone needs to be in charge of the strategy and execution to see to all the little details. If you have a small bar, it may be you. But marketing your bar or nightclub can be a full-time job—and as the owner of the establishment, you already have a full-time job (or several of them!).

If you have the means, you should consider hiring marketing help. It's especially important to hire someone else if you don't have a marketing background yourself, says Michael O'Harro, a board member of the National Bar and Restaurant Management Association. "I always had a full-time marketing person on my staff. In today's economy, it's especially important to sell yourself."

Dollar Stretcher

If you can't afford to hire marketing help, consider interns. Students at a local college may be willing to work for class credit. And they can give you a younger person's perspective on your bar.

Gerry Kelly, a nightclub marketing director himself, agrees in the importance of having a marketing staff. "Before you do anything else, you better have your marketing team together. Because having a fabulous location, regardless of where it is, and having it incredibly designed means nothing if you don't have the team to put it on the map."

If you don't have the budget to hire someone full time, you might consider a gregarious and on-the-ball bartender, DJ, or server to manage the promotions.

Marketing your bar and creating the buzz really lets you get creative. But before we get too far into the marketing process, let's start at the beginning . . . your bar's grand opening.

Hitting a Grand Slam

"The last thing you want to do is just open your doors and hope that the people will come," O'Harro says. "That's a risky situation."

Instead of hoping the people show up, you need to show them the way. People are always on the lookout for something new and exciting. As a result, grand openings tend to generate a great deal of interest for new businesses—as long as they're done right. Your opening night gives you a chance to make a memorable first impression on your guests. If they have a fantastic time at your bar the very first weekend, then they will not only come back, but they'll tell all their friends about you. On the other hand, if you don't plan and execute your grand opening to your customers' satisfaction, it can take months to recover from all the bad word-of-mouth advertising that may result.

When you're planning your grand opening, the first thing you need to do is come up with a strategy. Set a target date, and make it reasonable. If you've done all the marketing and footwork to get people interested in your grand opening, and you don't have all your licenses and permits by that date or you don't have enough staff, then you won't be able to open your doors. All your preliminary work will have gone to waste.

Once you've planned the theme, activities, promotions, specials, or whatever you want to do for your event, you can make a timeline to get everything done by working backward from your opening date. Here are six things you should include on your grand opening calendar:

1. Set a deadline for staff training prior to the grand opening, including a "dress rehearsal." You can invite friends and family of the staff, business contacts, and your suppliers to come to the free pre-opening. This gives you the opportunity to get some feedback and work out any glitches ahead of time.

Smart Tip

Tip...

If you can fit it into your budget, you might consider hiring a public relations firm to promote your grand opening. One club in New York City hired such a firm, which not only helped get celebrities to the event, but created 22 weeks of continuous press coverage in newspapers and magazines. The bar was a huge success from the very first night!

2. Test all equipment well in advance. If something needs repair, you want to have enough time to get it fixed before you open.

3. Work closely with government agencies to make sure your licenses and permits will be completed in plenty of time.

4. Make an ordering schedule with your suppliers well in advance of your opening date to make sure you're completely stocked.

5. Send out your marketing materials, such as direct mail, fliers, press releases, and advertisements.

6. Join your local chamber of commerce and/or other business associations to meet other business owners in the area.

Reaching the Right People

A popular way to develop a strong clientele at your grand opening (and a sure way to make it newsworthy) is to send out exclusive fliers or special invitations to key people who are in your community. O'Harro suggests developing a mailing list of the influential people in your area who will help spread the word and create a buzz about your bar.

"I would contact the local sports teams, flight attendants, local television personalities, and radio personalities," O'Harro says. "I'd find out who all the beautiful people were, along with the influential people, and I'd develop a mailing list. I would create a media buzz in the community, have a huge grand opening party—maybe even black tie—so the whole town would be talking about the place from day one."

You should also introduce yourself to nearby merchants and personally invite them to the grand opening. Other types of businesses sometimes have the opportunity to make recommendations to their customers. You can also benefit from a relationship with the local convention and tourism bureau.

The old saying "You never get a second chance to make a first impression" definitely applies to your bar's grand opening.

That means you don't want to open before you're ready. It's natural to want to begin your operation as soon as possible, even if it means serving customers while construction is going on behind you. "Most people who come to South Beach to open a club make the huge mistake of trying desperately to get open," says Gerry Kelly. "You're investing a great deal of money into the project, so it is better to have a competent marketing director who can advise you on the best time to open."

Bright Idea

Bob Brenlin, a neighborhood pub owner in Seattle, offers a great way to get a little more for your advertising dollar: "If you take any kind of ads out in a publication, you should ask them to send someone out to review your place."

Kelly says that the right marketing and preparation for your opening are "the bible of success for anyone in the nightlife industry. It's also the eternal failure of many operators. Money won't buy success; preparation will."

When planning your grand opening, Kelly suggests opening with a schedule of back-to-back events. "If you don't create the right kind of buzz, then you're just another beautiful venue with no one there."

Chances are, you'll make some mistakes at your grand opening, but hopefully your guests will be having such a great time that they won't notice them. This is your time to really shine and strut your stuff, so make the most of it. If you plan it right, you can kick off your business with grand style that brings you grand success!

Fanning the Flames

After your grand opening, the marketing doesn't stop there. One of the best ways to market your bar or nightclub is the internet. Most businesses today can—and do—benefit from e-marketing.

E-marketing doesn't have to involve a big campaign; you can start small, with just a website. Younger consumers, especially, spend plenty of time online and often use the internet as a place to research and compare eating and drinking establishments before selecting a place to go. Unless you or one of your staffers has a good deal of experience in building websites, you'll want to hire someone to design a site for you. It doesn't have to be terribly expensive, and the professional-looking results will be worth the money you spend.

When selecting a web designer, ask to see samples of candidates' work to make sure you like their style. You'll also want to discuss who will handle selecting and registering a domain name, and who will be hosting the site. Not all web designers host websites, but most can recommend companies who do. Another topic to discuss is site maintenance and updates: Your site should change frequently to list your promotions and specials, so you'll need to find out who will be able to make those changes.

In general, your website should include basic information about your establishment, including your hours of operation, location, contact information (such as a telephone number), types of payment accepted, and a sample of your menu—or even the entire thing. You should make sure the look and feel of your website fits with the theme you've selected for your bar.

In addition to providing information about your bar or club, your website should offer a way for your customers to contact you electronically. One way to do this is to include a form where customers can request information from you or provide feedback on their experiences there. You may also want to include a place where visitors can register to receive a newsletter or e-mails that advertise your specials.

A website is a great—and legal—way to provide information about your bar or nightclub, but the laws surrounding marketing alcohol online can be tricky. You should check with a lawyer who's knowledgeable in internet law before you decide to provide detailed information about any of the types of alcohol you serve.

Sending out newsletters and e-mails to regular customers, or advertising using services such as Google Adwords, are all effective e-marketing methods for bar and nightclub owners. But the best—and first—step that any bar or nightclub owner should take is building an attractive, easy-to-use, and easy-to-find website.

Special Events

In addition to e-marketing, you should constantly be planning promotions to keep the excitement going. Refer back to your market research and your concept to make sure you're staying on track with your original mission. Keep in mind that a "promotion" can be any type of event that brings business into your bar. Promotions can take place inside or outside your establishment.

Inside promotions include all the items you create with your bar's logo on them, such as napkins, coasters, glasses, T-shirts, hats, matches, buttons, bumper stickers, etc. Anything with your name and logo on it becomes an advertisement for your bar. You can get creative and match promotional items with your concept. For example, if you have a beach theme, you can sell or give away beach towels and Frisbees. Or if you have a fishing or boat theme, you can design tackle boxes with your name and logo on them. The possibilities are limitless. Have some fun with it!

Other inside promotions include happy hour, drink and food specials, theme nights, and other special events that take place inside the bar. (Remember that laws vary from city to city, so whenever you're planning an event, you should make sure it falls within the laws of your town.) Event promotions usually involve some sort of guest participation, which creates its own entertainment. You can build a whole set of promotions to go along with your themed events, such as giveaway items commemorating the event, contests, prizes, music designed to match the theme, and decorations throughout the bar that reflect the theme. If you're going to do a St. Patrick's Day event, you can decorate your bar in green, have a green beer special, play Irish music, give away prizes like T-shirts, logo beer mugs, and other items that celebrate the event, and whatever else you can dream up that goes along with the holiday.

It's All About Strategy

You can start planning your promotions calendar way in advance of the actual event. How far in advance you begin depends on the event, how extensively you want to promote it, and how long it will take to create the entertainment, prizes, etc. You should allow plenty of time to assess your needs and make clear, realistic goals.

Start Spreading the News . . .

If you have the budget, you can begin generating excitement for your bar's grand opening early in the game. Here are some ideas other bars have executed that worked like a charm:

○ *Two months before your grand opening, do a "teaser" campaign of billboards or newspaper ads.* The ads should say "(Your Bar) Is Coming On (Opening Date)" or "Watch for (Your Bar) On (Opening Date)."

○ *You can also run a teaser campaign online, using your website.* Use it to offer hints about your bar or club, much like movie studios do when trying to build buzz about upcoming movies.

○ *Create unique invitations that grab people's attention.* One bar designed a coaster with its logo on it and printed the invitation on the back. Another place sent out logo glasses (with the invitation rolled up inside) inviting guests to bring the glass in for a complimentary drink on opening night.

○ *Design a promotion to go along with your grand opening.* For example, a sports bar sent out football game schedules and half a season ticket stub to invited guests. If their half-ticket matched a ticket at the bar, they won season tickets to the local football team's games.

○ *Team up with a media partner to host an event on your opening night.* A nightclub partnered with MTV for a huge grand opening event that garnered national media coverage to the exact demographic it wanted to reach.

○ *Coordinate your grand opening with a charity event.* For instance, a bar and grill invited hundreds of prominent community members to its grand opening. The bar charged for drinks but gave the guests free food and donation envelopes for the National Children's Cancer Foundation. The charity received $5,000, and the bar was packed throughout the two-day event.

Once you've been in business awhile, you can evaluate your past promotions and decide what works and doesn't with your clientele. You'll also be able to get a better picture of your competition. What types of promotions are they running? What seems to work for them? What can you do to improve your competitive edge? If you're not doing as well as you would like to be, you can return to the market research phase. Set up focus groups and/or surveys to find out what your customers like and don't like about your bar. (See the "Customer Comment Card" on page 151.)

▲

Howdy, Partner

When creating promotions for your bar, you can often partner with other types of businesses who attract the same clientele as you. Depending on your target demographic, you may do a cross-promotion with any number of businesses. Here is a list of possible businesses to get your creative juices flowing:

Fitness center	Hair salon	Record store
Clothing shop	Sports memorabilia store	Video rental store
Car dealership	Shoe store	Electronics store
Stockbroker	Attorney	Accountant
Real estate agency	Travel agent	Restaurant
Movie theater	Playhouse	Symphony
Bookstore	Antique store	Nonprofit organization
Sports teams	Radio station	Television station

You can also develop an ongoing mailing list to remind your regular customers of the events and promotions you have coming up. Bar management consultant Bob Johnson recommends sending out a newsletter—either by postal mail or e-mail. "You might create a little newsletter that you send out once a month," says Johnson. "It would include a bunch of events coming up, as well as any specials you're going to be running. I'd include human interest articles about regular customers and employees."

You can also send out postcards or fliers to advertise your events and promotions. Developing a mailing list isn't as difficult as you might think. You can contact mailing houses that specialize in direct mail—they can narrow your list by zip code and demographics. You can also keep a fish bowl or other container at the bar or hostess stand for people to put their business cards in for a drawing to win a free drink or appetizer. Comment cards can work for you both as feedback and to help develop your mailing list.

The important thing to keep in mind when developing your marketing and promotion strategy is getting the most bang for your buck. If you have a talented writer and designer on your staff, you can give them an extra hourly

Bright Idea

Your wine list can do more than just list your wines. Instead of just listing the product, year, and price, you can include a brief description of the wine to help sell it. And if you serve food as well, you can suggest a entrée that will complement the wine.

Customer Comment Card

At the 49th Street Bar & Grill, we want to make sure you're completely satisfied with your experience. To help us serve you better, please answer the following questions:

1. Is this your first visit?   ❏ Yes   ❏ No

2. If you are a returning customer, about how many times have you been here in the past month? (please circle one)

    2 or fewer   3–5   6–10   11–15   16–20   21 or more

3. How would you rate your overall experience?
    ❏ Poor   ❏ Fair   ❏ Average   ❏ Good   ❏ Very Good

4. How would you rate the quality of your drinks?
    ❏ Poor   ❏ Fair   ❏ Average   ❏ Good   ❏ Very Good

5. How would you rate the food quality?
    ❏ Poor   ❏ Fair   ❏ Average   ❏ Good   ❏ Very Good

6. How would you rate the service you received?
    ❏ Poor   ❏ Fair   ❏ Average   ❏ Good   ❏ Very Good

7. How do you like the atmosphere of the 49th Street Bar & Grill?
    ❏ Poor   ❏ Fair   ❏ Average   ❏ Good   ❏ Very Good

8. What did you think of the entertainment?
    ❏ Poor   ❏ Fair   ❏ Average   ❏ Good   ❏ Very Good

9. What radio stations do you listen to most often?_____

10. What newspaper do you read most often?_____

11. Other comments:_____

    _____

    _____

    _____

    _____

Name:_____

Address:_____

City:_____ State:_____ Zip:_____

Birthday:_____ Wedding anniversary:_____

▲

wage to oversee the newsletter and come up with all the stories. Use the resources you have at your disposal. Sometimes your employees have more insight than an outside agency as to what your customers would be interested in reading about in a newsletter. Most of the entrepreneurs we interviewed put almost no money into traditional advertising. But they set aside about 10 percent of their sales for marketing and promotions.

Corralling All Your Resources

When you're getting ready to plan a promotion, keep in mind that you're not the only one who benefits from your bar's success. Your suppliers benefit, and the companies that produce the alcohol you sell benefit, too. Since everyone involved understands this concept, you can team up with beer and alcohol companies to help sponsor your events. Talk to your suppliers to find out your options.

You can also work with other types of businesses to create cross-promotions. Once you begin to see the potential of tie-ins with your bar, the possibilities can grow exponentially. When you talk to other businesses about possible cross-promotions, let them know how both businesses will benefit and focus on what the promotion will do for them. You can inform them about your clientele and tell them how many people you have in the bar on an average night, week, and month. Their business will be mentioned in all promotional materials and maybe even by your DJs and in your newsletter. In return, they can supply the prizes, offer discount specials, and/or help with the cost of the promotion itself. Generally, you'll want them to provide something like a prize or giveaway item as an incentive to draw people in on the night of the promotion.

If you work with a DJ, he or she should mention upcoming promotions two to three times per hour to remind your customers of the next promotion coming up. Remind your DJs to keep the announcements short (20 seconds or fewer), and to refrain from talking over the vocals in a song. If you have televisions hooked up to a video system, you can create your own commercials that you can run a few times every hour, too.

You can also use your own resources to promote your business and drive sales. Table tents on each table and on the bar can advertise drink specials, happy hour specials, or food specials. If you have a menu, use it to your advantage. You

Bright Idea

For holidays and other special events, most of your competitors will be hosting some sort of promotion as well. Think of something that will make yours different. For example, instead of scheduling your Super Bowl party in the late afternoon when the game is about to start, begin your promotion a couple hours earlier—before all the other bars get going.

can strategically place small-space ads on your menu to highlight certain food items or drinks. If you put a box around the ad and make it a different color, it will grab customers' attention.

Remember that your menu is an excellent marketing tool. Placing certain items in specific areas on the menu will get the most attention. See "Hey, Look Here!" below for the top five attention-grabbing areas of your menu.

Hey, Look Here!		
Your Menu		
3rd most visible		2nd most visible
	Prime ad space (1st most visible)	
4th most visible		5th most visible

Get the Ball Rolling

Once you've established what your promotions will be, it's time to start making them happen. After you bar is up and running, you'll have a better idea of what nights need a little boost. Most bars are busy on Friday and Saturday nights, with Thursdays coming in third place. You might decide you need to pump up business on Monday or Tuesday, so pick one day and keep it going until you've established enough regular business to move the promotions to a different day. Of course, you'll still do your holiday promotions, like July 4th, Super Bowl, Cinco de Mayo, etc., on the appropriate days.

Here are some ideas to keep in mind when you're working on promotional events:

- *Prepare*. Work out a budget. If your promotion continues for more than one day, budget for the entire time you want it to run. A good goal to shoot for is to make a profit that's three times the cost of the promotion.
- *Make a schedule*. Design a planning calendar at least eight weeks before the promotion. Depending on the size and magnitude of the promotion, you may want

A Reason to Party

Following is a list of many events, special occasions, and possible promotions you may see celebrated in a bar. Your choices, not only which occasions you celebrate but how you promote them, should come from the overall concept you want your bar to represent.

Mardi Gras	Stanley Cup Playoffs
Kentucky Derby	Dance Contests
St. Patrick's Day	Spring Break
Groundhog Day	Earth Day Celebration
Mark Twain's Birthday	Cinco de Mayo
April Fool's Day	Indy 500
July 4th	New York in the 1920s
'70s Disco	Ping-Pong Tournament
Art Exhibitions	Beach Party
New Year's Eve	Olympics
Taco Tuesdays	Mother's Day
Thanksgiving	Father's Day
Moon Landing Anniversary	Darts Tournament
Pool Tournament	Toga Party
Karaoke	Amateur Comedy Night
World Series	Baby Picture Party
Disney Night	Fashion Auction
Ugly Tie Day	Casino Night
Lincoln's Birthday	Elvis Presley Night
Super Bowl	Rocky Horror Picture Show
Election Day	Charlie Brown (Peanuts) Night
Halloween	Valentine's Day
The Boston Tea Party	

First Day of Summer, Winter, Spring, and/or Autumn

Broadway Bash (come as characters in different musicals)

Dress Up as Your Favorite _____ Night

to start advertising it at this point, too. Avoid advertising an ending date, though, so you can cut it early if it doesn't do as well as you planned or you can extend it if it really takes off.

- *Maintain the energy level.* On the day of the promotion, don't stop the action to give away prizes or make announcements. You can turn the music down, but don't turn it off. This will keep the energy level high and consistent. If you absolutely have to turn off the music, never keep it off for more than 10 minutes, or you risk people getting impatient and leaving.

- *Party all night.* Schedule your prize giveaways, contests and entertainment to run throughout the night. If you have a grand prize to give away or a finale planned, don't do it until after midnight so your guests stay in your bar as late as possible.

Promoting your bar can be fun and creative. During a promotion and after it's over, ask your customers and your employees for feedback and critiques. Of course, your sales will give you a lot of the information you're looking for, too. On page 154, you will find some ideas for promotions that might spark your own imagination. Go crazy!

In Chapter 13, we'll dive into controlling your finances once your bar is up and running. By keeping efficient records and managing your profits, you have a better chance for success as you go from a fledgling operation to a bar business veteran.

The Numbers Game:
Financial Management

Now you have a pretty good idea of how to get your bar started and have discovered some ways to improve your business once you've opened. In this chapter, we're going to get down and dirty. Once you've opened your doors, we want your bar to be one that succeeds. We're going to delve into the

▲

number-crunching end of the business and give you some tips on how to make sure you not only stay afloat but become a huge success!

Bookkeeping, accounting, financial management, and keeping up with your taxes are all key ingredients to your recipe for success. You can have the hottest bar in town, but if you're not managing your finances correctly, you can end up losing it all.

Pay special attention to the information on income statements, balance sheets, and cash-flow statements. You'll want to refer to these three financial reports any time you make decisions about your business. Your income statement will give you a picture of your revenue, costs, expenses, and profits, while your balance sheet—which details your assets and your liabilities—will provide a snapshot of where your business stands financially at any given time. The cash-flow statement will show you where your money is coming from and where it's going, as well as the status of your investments and financing.

Crunching the Numbers

Besides giving you a look at your financial position and where your money is being spent, your income statement can show you how certain categories relate to each other. For example, you can figure out what percentage you're spending on food vs. alcohol. Or you can see your net profit in terms of actual dollars and in percentages. You can also compare your income statements to find out if your business is making more or less money than, say, six months ago. This is very important for any business, but especially to a bar business.

You may discover that during the same period last year you sold more alcohol than food, and this year, you're selling more food than alcohol. You need to find out why and may need to make some changes to resolve the difference. Your income statement may also tell you that your costs have increased, but your sales have remained the same. This would also require some investigating and problem-solving.

If you ask the right questions, you can find solutions to the challenges reflected in your income statement before they become too big to handle. The problem may be as simple as carelessness or inadequate training. These kinds of issues are relatively easy to solve if you catch them before your business gets into real

> **Tip...**
>
> **Smart Tip**
> If your financial statements show that you're having some trouble spots, but you can't pin down the problem, you might consider bringing in a consultant. A consultant will usually spend a few weeks analyzing your bar until they figure out what's going wrong. Then they'll help you come up with solutions to get you back on track.

trouble. Your accountant will be able to help you analyze your financial statements, but you can help, too. When you're looking at your income statement, ask yourself the following questions to see if you can catch any trouble spots:

- *What is the relation of costs to sales?* Has there been any significant change since the last statement? Why?
- *How do your expenses match up with other bars in your area?* (This is a great question to ask your accountant!)
- *Are your sales improving?* If not, why not?
- *Look back at your previous income statements.* Do you see any new trends emerging?
- *What was the biggest surprise to you on your income statement?* Why was it significant?

As you begin to ask yourself and your accountant questions about your income statement, you may uncover problems you had no idea existed. Once you find them, you can start working with your management team to come up with some solutions.

Finding the Control Zone

Only you can decide the right amount of control you want to have over your bar. If you're an active owner who's always on the premises, you may not need as many controls since you'll have a day-to-day knowledge of what's going on in your establishment. On the other hand, if you're an absentee owner who depends on your management to protect your investment, you might want to have a tighter rein.

Whatever your situation, you don't want to put control mechanisms in place that cost more money than they save. However, even if you're an active owner, you want to have a certain amount of controls in place so you don't reach the point of not being able to trust your managers and employees if you're not there to watch them. Controls help give you some peace of mind when you can't be there every minute. Most are simple and don't require too much effort.

Depending on your business, you can monitor your food and beverage costs daily, weekly, or monthly. You don't want to go more than a month without knowing where your numbers stand. You may find that your bartenders are free-pouring drinks or giving away drinks, and that's the reason your pour-cost percentage is going up. That's an easy fix. Or you might end up having to do some investigating to find out why your costs are rising. It's better to know what's going on early, before it starts doing serious harm to your business.

Your weekly and monthly cost percentages are going to give you an idea of what kind of trends your business is experiencing. Hopefully, your trends will reflect higher sales and flat costs! If you decide to calculate your costs on a daily basis, don't put too

▲

much weight on them individually. You're going to have good days and bad days. It's the nature of the business. For example, if someone accidentally drops a bottle of liquor one night, your pour-cost percentage (PC%) is going to be unusually high for that day. But when you look at it again in your weekly or monthly report, it won't have such a great effect. If you see trends of rising costs in your weekly reports, keep an eye on them and start trying to figure out why. If they show up again in your monthly reports, it's time to take action.

Size Can Make a Difference

Besides your level of involvement as an owner, the size of your bar may play a big role in how many controls you should have in place. If you have a small bar, you may decide to implement a limited number of controls. Our experts recommend having at least some minimal controls in place, no matter how small your bar or how great your

---

Don't Speed through That Yellow Light!

When you're analyzing the success of your business, look for certain signals that scream "Caution!" The following items will help you determine your strengths and point out areas where you need improvement:

○ *Pour-cost percentage (PC%).* We talked about this formula in Chapter 9, but it's a figure you'll use constantly when determining the health of your bar.

○ *Food-cost percentage.* Similar to the PC%, this will tell you what percentage of a food item's price goes to the cost of the ingredients. To figure out the percentage, use the following formula: food-cost percentage = cost of food sold ÷ food sales.

○ *Labor-cost percentage.* This gives you the percentage of your sales that goes to labor cost. To figure the percentage, use this formula: labor-cost percentage = (payroll + benefits) ÷ total sales.

○ *Average guest check.* Find out how much each of your customers spends at your bar. This amount may help you uncover problems with service or quality. If this number is low, you might have a contest among your employees for the person who has the highest guest check average for a week. Many ordering systems will give you this amount automatically. If yours doesn't, you can figure it out with this formula: average guest check = total sales ÷ number of guests served.

Bright Idea

Schedule meetings with your managers to discuss your monthly cost reports. If your costs are on target, you'll have the opportunity to praise them for a job well done. If your reports signal some problems, you can discuss them as a team and try to find out the cause and the solution.

involvement. The absolute minimum number of controls you have should include a scheduled inventory check (weekly or monthly), sales records, and purchase (cost) records. These will help you keep track of your PC% and your food-cost percentages.

If you run a large club or bar, you'll want to have more controls in place. Even if you're on the premises every hour your bar is open, you can't be everywhere in a large bar. You will also have more areas of business to oversee. You may have a situation where five different promoters are putting together a themed night with different clientele Sunday through Thursday. You could have a country music night, a techno dance night, a retro night, a rock 'n' roll night, etc. That means you have to keep track of how each of those nights is doing individually, as well as the cost and sales of your bar or club as a whole. It can start to get complicated rather quickly if you don't have some controls in place.

For large bars or clubs, you may need to conduct daily inventories, which will then translate into both your weekly and monthly inventories. You may also decide to implement other controls, such as waste sheets, sales analysis by type of alcohol, and reports detailing the cost of happy hour vs. nighttime sales. A liquor sales analysis can not only help you determine cost vs. sales, but it can also predict the trends that happen in your bar. By breaking down the sales into liquor, draft beer, domestic bottled beer, imported bottled beer, wine, and food, you can follow buying trends over each month at a glance. You still have your inventory and ordering to see exactly where your sales are coming from, but the monthly analysis gives you a more general report for a larger bar or club.

If you end up having more than one location, even more controls need to be established. Again, you don't want to go overboard and become a control freak. You can start with the minimal controls and add more as you see fit—depending on where you're seeing problems in your cost percentages. If you start out with a large-sized bar, or if you grow into one, the importance of communication with your staff increases exponentially with your size. Communicate with your managers about costs and sales. They may need to communicate with

Smart Tip

Professional associations keep track of statistical data on operating costs and offer it to their members. The National Restaurant Association (restaurant.org) can help you find out how your bar's expenditures compare to the national averages for your size and type.

your bartenders as well. You don't have to restrict the dialogue to negative news, either. If your cost percentages are doing well, let them know that you appreciate their professionalism and attention to detail.

Patrolling Your People

The theory behind police patrol doesn't involve going out on the streets to bust people. The police go out on patrol to maintain order for the safety of the community. In a sense, you must adopt this theory for your bar. Patrol your managers, servers, and bartenders to maintain order for the safety and success of your business. You don't have to be militant about it, but you should keep an eye out for habits or practices that could hurt your business.

There are many, many ways employees and managers can steal from your business, and it's not always money they're taking. Food and alcohol are also hot commodities. Make sure you and your managers keep a watchful eye out for habits that could result in lost sales or profits for your bar. Here are some things to look out for when patrolling your staff:

- Trying to cover up alcohol shortages by adding water to liquor bottles, or pouring well liquor into empty premium bottles
- Giving free drinks to friends or other employees
- Drinking alcohol (for free, of course) while working behind the bar
- Creating lost guest checks, breakage, or petty cash payouts to pocket the money
- Keeping the cash drawer open and only ringing up a certain number of sales
- Overpouring or heavy pouring to get better tips from customers
- Short pouring (pouring less for some customers to make up for overpouring for other customers)
- Taking gifts from suppliers for purchasing their merchandise without reporting them to you. This may result in overordering or clouded judgment on getting competitive prices.
- Serving well drinks to customers and charging them for premium drinks
- Fake overrings (reringing the tab for a lower amount after a customer leaves, then pocketing the difference)

Theft is a major reason why your PC% could get out of control.

Sometimes, bar owners develop a "free drink policy" for their guests and employees. Bartenders and servers are allowed to give out a certain number of complimentary drinks to regular customers or friends each night (as long as this is allowed in your city or town). This policy can help generate goodwill for your regular customers—

they'll feel special. Your employees will also benefit from the policy, as free drinks often translate into better tips.

However, if you decide to adopt this policy, you should implement some kind of control to prevent abuse. Some employees will say they gave out their allotted free drinks, but they actually charged for them and kept the money. This doesn't benefit your bar or your customers. If you decide to have a free drink policy in your bar, you should have a manager sign off on all free drinks and document the reason for giving them out. If all your free drinks are going to your employees' friends, the policy isn't really helping you improve your sales.

Automated Pour-Cost Policing

One way to prevent theft and bad serving habits is by using an automated dispensing system. These systems can be as simple as a bottle pour spout with a built-in counting device or as complicated as a fully automated dispenser that pours just the right amount of alcohol at the touch of a button. Depending on your bar's volume and your budget, you may decide to install some sort of dispensing system.

According to manufacturers of automatic dispensing systems, they'll give your customers perfectly blended cocktails, and they'll give you better pour-cost percentages. These systems have a downside, though. Many customers enjoy watching bartenders flipping the bottles up and down while their drinks are being made. Your guests may find an automated dispensing system impersonal and think that you're a miser because you have one. Another factor that you should consider is the expense. These systems can cost anywhere from $2,000 to $10,000 and more per station. Some of the systems are integrated into cash registers for even more detail and automation. However, if the cost isn't going to be more than covered by the amount it will save you, it's not going to be worth it for your bar.

From Preventive to Proactive

Preventive measures can help you stay in business. But as a bar owner, you don't just want to stay in business—you want to be a raging success! To keep increasing your sales, you'll need to be proactive. You can do little things like improving food quality, adding new items, and creating new and innovative drink recipes and specials. But how are you going to keep those creative juices flowing when you're busy with the day-to-day operations?

As in any other industry, you need to keep up with the latest trends in the bar business. You should subscribe to every bar-related publication and try to visit related websites whenever you get a chance. If you're a dance club or have live music in your bar, you need to keep on top of the latest music trends, too. Subscribe to music magazines like *Billboard* to stay on top of who's hot and who's not. Some cities have local entertainment publications, too. These publications can give you a great deal of insight into what's going on in your community and what interests your clientele. You can often pick up ideas for promotions by linking an event at your bar with something that's happening in your area. If you run a sports bar, you should have subscriptions to a few sports magazines. You also want to take

advantage of all the free resources online, too. You can stay on top of the hot new music and bar trends online, without paying for a subscription to a magazine.

Joining associations can help keep you connected to other bar owners as well. You may come across another bar owner who has faced the same challenges you're facing. You can benefit from their experience by finding out how they solved their problem. Associations also have trade shows and conventions that offer seminars on topics directly related to your business. You can find out what's happening in the bar business on a larger scale. You can also find out about the latest technologies in equipment that might help make your job easier or even make you more money.

The Benefits of Upselling

Your number-one priority as a business owner is to improve your sales. By encouraging your staff to upsell your customers to call brands or premium brands, you'll increase your profits. For example, if a customer orders a vodka and tonic from your bartender, your bartender should respond with "Will that be Absolut or Stolichnaya?" If someone orders a rum and coke, your server can then ask "Would you like Bacardi 151 or Captain Morgan?" If two people at a table order the same kind of draft beer, your staff can suggest they buy a pitcher instead.

Customers don't always think about these things when they order a drink, even if they prefer a certain brand or would rather have a pitcher. Your employees should remind them. Upselling increases your average guest check and your profit margins. Of course, it will also increase your PC%, but it is a positive increase. Here's a comparison between a well-brand and a call-brand order:

Cost of well-brand rum = $0.25 per shot

Well drink price = $3.25

PC% = 7.7%

Gross profit = $3.00

Cost of call-brand rum = $0.65 per shot

Call drink price = $4.25

PC% = 15.3%

Gross profit = $3.60

As you can see, the higher PC% doesn't reflect lower profit. Train your employees to upsell their customers. You can even offer incentives for the bartender or server who has the highest average guest check to encourage them to boost those sales. And of course, higher sales translate into better tips for them, too!

We've given you a lot of information about starting and running a bar in this book, but you can never learn everything there is to know about the bar business. You've gotten this far, so you know the value of educating yourself about your business. Don't stop now! Make it your goal to keep learning about running a bar for as long as you own one (or maybe, eventually, a whole chain!). Knowledge can be a very powerful tool for success.

Now you have the map you need to not only keep your bar on track with financial statements and control mechanisms but to increase your sales and keep your business growing, too. In the next chapter, we'll talk about the challenges and triumphs bar owners have faced as they reached for the same goals you will. The bar owners and industry experts who generously helped with this book were once where you are now. In the following chapter, they're going to tell you the secrets to success and reasons for failure in the bar business so you know what to look for before you get started.

14

Words of
Wisdom

Now it's time to do a little cheerleading.
Statistics on success and failure in the bar business can't give
you the real information you need to succeed. Talking to individual bar owners and finding out their real-life challenges and triumphs will give you much more insight than percentage points
on paper. Before you get started, have some conversations with

a few successful bar owners. Delve into their stories. Uncover their secrets to success. These discussions will provide a great deal of insight as to what kinds of problems you may encounter on your own quest to operate a successful establishment.

In this concluding chapter, we're going to let the entrepreneurs and experts we interviewed give you their best advice. We'll revisit some of the most common mistakes made in this industry. Remember: Hindsight really is 20/20, so try to imagine what, if any, challenges or problems your decisions might cause before you make them final. Next, you'll read some encouraging stories of well-thought-out decisions and the favorable results they've given bar owners. In addition, they will tell you what they would go back and change if they could.

The Obstacle Course

The reasons for failure in this industry can be put into two categories: inadequate knowledge of the business and insufficient operating funds. Knowledge and experience in the bar industry prove extraordinarily helpful when hiring, training, and managing your staff. They'll enhance your ability to deal with the issues, both strategic and emergent, that you will face as a bar owner. "I think that people who get into the bar business who haven't been in the business are asking to fail," says Michael O'Harro, a board member of the National Bar & Restaurant Management Association.

If you have some experience in the bar or nightclub industry, you'll be more accustomed to the lifestyle. As Bob Brenlin, the neighborhood bar owner in Seattle, points out, "Even when you set hours for yourself, you'll end up working seven days a week. There's no doubt that you'll be getting calls late at night, or coming down on Sunday to deal with problems." Understanding this, and finding ways to negotiate your own life and the life of your bar, comes with knowledge and experience.

If you overspend and run out of money, you can sink the mightiest of businesses. Surprise costs pop up everywhere and for everyone—no matter how many bars they've run successfully. Our experts and owners strongly suggest you budget for at least 30 percent more money than your highest estimates say you'll need to begin your bar business. As we discussed in Chapter 9, every day will present new obstacles to your general manager (even if it's you) for negotiation. Whoever you trust to call the shots will have to make decisions, and stick by them, when it comes to every aspect of the operation. It should appear as if the flow of the business needs no management whatsoever. But to attain that appearance, every inconsistency and abnormality has to be discovered and corrected. Many of these "little things" will be caught and fixed by your staff, unless, of course, they're caused by your staff.

Mistaking Yourself Out of Business

Making 20 wrong decisions could put your business in a tough spot, but it may survive. Then again, making one significant mistake could render your operation bankrupt. It depends on what risks you take, how quickly you spot a mistake, and what steps you take to correct the error. Again, knowledge is your best friend when it comes to running a successful bar. Ron Newman, the sports bar owner in Manhattan Beach, California, says, "Let's say a person retires and decides they want to open a bar. If they're able to open it and make it work without having any experience, they must have great common sense. But even with that common sense, they're going to make a lot of mistakes. They might make it, but it's going to cost them a great deal because there are just so many things they don't know about."

When opening and running a bar, the most frequent mistakes owners make involve inventory control, managing and training staff, and matching the personality of the decision maker with the concept and targeted personality of the bar. Other high-problem areas include spreading your resources too thin by overspending or underselling, and fixating on the negatives of the present or the past without an eye to future solutions.

Maintaining Steady Control

From purchasing supplies to selling goods, the control of your inventory will deeply affect your profits. Choose your purveyors carefully and keep them as honest as you can. Create specifications for each product. How much will you carry of what? Sometimes you'll need to update your original pars (the number of backup bottles you keep on hand). If you make changes, keep a file or log of when and why the change occurred so you can refer to it over time and keep track of the progress of your business.

Encourage your staff to make drinks and food according to standard recipes as instructed during training. Test your bartenders periodically to make sure they're sticking to the agreed-upon standards. Make sure every drink is accounted for in accordance with your policies. Whether a drink or food dish was sent back, made improperly, or given away for free, everything should be registered somewhere. If

Bright Idea

Put a chalkboard or a clipboard in the kitchen or office that has a list of the daily specials—for both drink and food. If you have a kitchen, you might place it near the pass shelf, to which both the cooks and servers have access. The shift's manager, with help from the lead cook and the bartender, will update the board when items are running low or are no longer available.

you have inventory-control problems, you'll need to refer to your established reports to figure out the problem.

Coaching Your Team

Your establishment will live or die by how professionally your customers are served and how much they feel like your guests. Your staff will wilt or prosper depending on the consistency and viability of the support given to them by your management team. Your service staff will assist your managers in getting to know your customers both as individuals and as a group. The better you and your employees know your customers, the better you can serve them.

Managers often ignore staff problems, hoping they'll just go away. However, most of the time the issues fester and eventually explode. The primary reason many managers don't get involved with interstaff problems is due to their fear of the explosion. However, it's always better to identify and solve problems before they interfere with your business or start to affect your customers.

Who's In Charge Here?

If you're the one who calls the shots for your operation, you'll have to keep abreast of what works and what doesn't. One very good, but very difficult, way to find out if your bar has the personality you want and is running properly is to visit during peak hours as a customer. You might bring a friend or colleague in for a drink and sit at a table to get a feel for what a customer experiences. In these situations, leave your knowledge of the bar at the door. Try to take in the furnishings, decorations, and selections as if you walked into the bar for the first time.

As the decision maker, you so intimately know your bar's operation that you may find it difficult to act like a customer. One way to overcome this is to listen unobtrusively to the guests around you. What are they saying about the place, the service, the food, the drinks? Basically, keep your ears open. You should also watch your staff interact with each other and the customers.

From the moment people walk in your door, they start to develop impressions of your establishment. Do employees ignore the customers? Or do they greet them and try to make them feel welcome right away? If you're an active owner, you may end up standing around a lot—

Smart Tip

Tip...

No matter how approachable you think you are, your mere authority will intimidate some of your employees. Quiet, observant staff members may be able to give you some insight into your bar's problems. You may want to have a suggestion box to encourage your employees (or your guests) to come forward with their ideas.

like the lead hand on a cattle drive—waiting for something to go wrong so you can fix it. You'll experience a totally different point of view of how your guests are treated if you're sitting at a table like any other customer and allow yourself to be treated as such.

Of course, your employees won't just forget who you are. Your server will try to impress you, but you should pay more attention to how the other guests are treated. You may decide to change little things in your bar's appearance after sitting as a guest for an evening. What you think your bar says to its customers may not be what it's actually communicating. If this happens, it's more difficult to catch it and improve it if you are stuck obliviously inside it. So try to change your vantage point periodically.

Spreading Yourself Too Thin

Spreading your resources too thin creates major pitfalls and causes many bars to fail. The most common and obvious culprit is financing: You don't start with enough capital, you spend it on the wrong things, or you pay too much for equipment. The financial woes of this industry can snowball at any time, so be prepared with backup capital. The flip side is very true, as well: The financial gains in the bar business can snowball and cover you with glee.

Finances are not the only resource you must be careful with. Your employees can also be spread too thin. Your bar's business will fluctuate depending on the weather, time of year, and a host of other variables. Often, bar owners overwork their employees to the point of exhaustion. When your employees are overworked, they can become cranky and short-tempered, and their job performance and customer service will almost definitely suffer. This industry is filled with employees who live from day to day with their own personal finances. At any moment, one of them might decide not to show up for work tomorrow. You can safeguard against this to some extent during the hiring process by checking references, but keep in mind that happy, satisfied employees are less likely to start acting flaky.

One way to keep your employees happy and loyal is to be aware of their work schedules. For example, if Julie bartends every Friday and Saturday night for the first three months she works for you, and then you change her shifts to Wednesday and Thursday afternoons without

Dollar Stretcher

Many of the patterns in the bar business are seasonal and cyclical. Keep track of how much you sell and what you sell. If you run out of a particular product, document it and include the reason why. If you could sell $1,000 worth more of the beer you've run out of every three-day weekend, that could add up to a lot of extra money earned each year.

notice or explanation, you may find that her demeanor and attitude change drastically. Even though she's working the same amount of time, her income has probably decreased to such an extent that her mind is consumed with it. She may feel the need to get a different job or even a second job. If she starts directing her attention elsewhere, her performance at your bar will suffer, and you may even lose her altogether. Talk to your employees if you have to make major scheduling changes; explain your reasons and let them know if it's a temporary or permanent change.

Being a Cockeyed Optimist

When solving problems, we often focus on the problem itself, constantly thinking about the negatives. This adds up to living in the past because you focus on "not allowing this to happen again." Instead, direct your focus toward deciding what you want to happen and why. This mind-set will make the goal a positive, time-saving, or profit-making step that will encourage your employees to achieve it. Ask yourself: What's the best path to achieve my goals? If you look at the solution as something to

---

Sweet Charity

Giving freely to your community can create a positive reputation for your bar. You may want to donate goods, perhaps cups and napkins with your logo on them, to a charity picnic. Or you may just want to donate money. In other cases, you'll want to give your time to a cause or group that's doing something you believe in.

As an entrepreneur, you'll be bombarded by different charities to lend your support to. Investigate the nonprofit organizations and choose which will be equally beneficial to both the charity and your business. Let's face it: You're not going to have a lot of time or resources. If you don't already know the charitable causes to which you wish to contribute, then simply ask a representative to give you the information you want to know.

Michael O'Harro, a board member of the National Bar & Restaurant Management Association, says charity events are an excellent way to get exposure for your bar. "You've got to get involved in your city," says O'Harro. "It's a good idea to become a member of the citizens' association or the business association in your community. It will help you find out what's going on locally. Another benefit of getting involved with charities is you look like a good guy."

---

accomplish instead of a problem you have to avoid, you'll find your attitude, and the attitudes of your employees, will stay fresh, focused, and hopeful.

A Hard Day's Night

By now, you've probably discussed with your friends and family your desire to own a bar. Unless you've worked in this industry for years and proved that you can run a successful bar and still live a normal life, friends and family will probably jokingly say goodbye to you. Such is the power of the legend of how much time it takes to do this right. The family members who don't get to help out at the bar never get to spend time with you because you'll be obsessed with running the bar.

These rumors are based solidly in fact and aren't necessarily specific to the bar industry. All entrepreneurs are distracted by the weight of their investments. This distraction can get easily tagged as obsessive behavior by your family members and others vying for your attention. It's a sacrifice many entrepreneurs have to make to be successful. Make sure everyone involved is prepared for your lack of free time—including you.

On the plus side, the time you spend running your business, even during your heaviest periods, will speed by. You'll spend your time talking to people, making decisions, deciphering problems, and watching the flow of your operation. Hopefully, all those things will bring you joy. You should love running your business, or you shouldn't do it. This is not to say it will be easy or that you have to like every aspect of it, but yes . . . you have to love this business. The fact that this is your bar should make you very proud. That feeling makes it worth all the hours you give to it.

However, you don't have to let your bar take over your life. If you design your business' structure to allow the major decision maker two days off per week, then, for the most part, that's how it should go. Often (some say always), the owner and general manager will stop at the bar on their day off for a few minutes. You might want to take the bank deposit or finish up some paperwork. You can still consider that a day off. If you end up having to deal with problems or take over for the manager, then it's no longer a day off. This doesn't only happen to you and your general manager (who could also be you), but it may happen to all the managers you employ.

> **Tip...**
>
> ## Smart Tip
> The bar business is a nighttime business. If you want to make money selling alcohol, you'll most often sell it at night. If you manage your bar, then you'll have to work at night, too. If your spouse works during the day, make sure you discuss your potential schedule and overall time investment thoroughly with him or her before you invest.

Avoiding Starting Over Again

The choices you make will determine your overall goal and your bar's mission and concept. If you decide you made a mistake with the original concept and mission you chose, yet you're still in business, then you pretty much have to start brainstorming and choose again. Those decisions you wish you could make over again may be significant—like your concept—or they may be something easy to fix. According to the entrepreneurs we interviewed, one very good way to avoid crippling trouble is to have enough startup capital. Bob Brenlin puts it bluntly: "Have enough money going in so you can withstand the first few months of less-than-projected income. A lot of people go into it without enough money. It always costs more to do the project, so there'd better be a big chunk left over to take care of the first few months."

When you do get your business up and running, you can prevent many mistakes by putting efficient and practical controls in place. R.C. Colvin, the bar owner in Niles, Michigan, says, "In any business, you're going to make mistakes, but in the bar business it's even more important to really stay on top of your accounting and hold people responsible. You've got to have a liquor-monitoring program, and you have to be on top of your product."

If you know what you want from your operation in terms of sales of food and liquor, then you can plan for what you need to reach your goals. Tell your experts and your staff what you want, and consider all their suggestions. Of course, you'll make a lot of decisions before you have a staff to help you figure it out. For example, the size of your kitchen and the type of equipment you should have will need to be decided before you're up and running.

Determining the identity of your bar isn't nearly as easy as it sounds. You'll probably change aspects of your bar's personality often, sometimes without even knowing it. To work your way out of an identity crisis, you must note what's going on around you and take advantage of all opportunities. Rely on your consultants and experts. Talk to other owners and do lots of your own research.

Ron Newman says he would have done more to prepare to grow with other locations. "I'd make sure we used systems that we could expand with, systems we could use in a chain operation," says Newman. "We didn't even think about it when we first started, but I definitely

Bright Idea

Knowledge is a valuable tool for any business owner. Use the resources in the Appendix of this book to amass all the information you can about the bar business. Read trade magazines, talk to industry associations, or call some of our experts. The more you know, the better chance you have of putting your feet firmly on the path to success.

see the benefit of it now." Even if you only have one location, he says, you still need good systems to ensure that your business is profitable.

After joking that you should "think twice," Brenlin gives this advice to new bar owners: "It has to be a labor of love—you're probably not going to make a lot of money. You need to be able to go small, easy to control, which will make a difference on whether you make any money. There are all kinds of risks when you get larger, so you better have a good location, a strong lease, a good business plan, and solicit as many people as possible. Then market the heck out of the place."

Triumphs of the Trade

Every project has its highs and lows, victories and struggles. The trick is to learn from both without taking anything for granted. You've just been reminded of the major mistakes made in this business. Now you'll uncover some of the victories and pleasantries this industry offers its owners.

As a bar owner, you're not only working toward your own financial security but also providing a livelihood for your employees. How's that for satisfying? But from day to day, you need to have a reason to do this job, beyond just money.

Colvin bought his bar because he loves to shoot pool. But another source of fun he's found is learning new things. "It had been more than 20 years since I'd done my own accounting," he says. "The software changed a lot, so it's kind of like I went back to kindergarten. I spent a lot of time in the back room learning how to make my forms with Excel and doing my accounting."

Kelly acknowledges the great stress of his job. "When you have a cell phone and people know the number, the work never stops," he laments. "If you don't answer that call at 10 o'clock at night, well, guess what—your competitor is getting the business." But he also sees the upside. "Owning a club, or running a club, is probably the closest thing to being a rock star—people look at you like a celebrity."

Ron Newman thinks his partnership with his son is one of his greatest triumphs. Although Newman had owned a chain of successful bars himself, his son convinced him to come out of retirement and start another bar as a partnership. "For our situation, the best thing was the dynamic between myself and my son," says Newman. "I was lucky that he was better than me in many areas. He brought youth and his creativity. I brought experience and my own creativity. So I learned a whole different way of doing business. We are like a musician and a lyricist. We make a great team."

Kelly says his single biggest accomplishment "was getting Bill Clinton to host an event in 2002. Learning the protocol with the Secret Service and how to treat a

What If You Beat the Odds?

So you've done it. You've started a bar business whose prosperity rivals the most famously successful bars in the land. What now? Basically, you have four choices: Expand, stay the same, franchise, or sell.

1. *Expand.* Before you decide to expand, ask three questions: Why? How? And where? Usually the answer to the first question will follow a problem, like not having enough space for the throngs of people coming to your bar. The answers to the next two questions are more difficult. Do you have the physical space for the equipment needed to expand or to open another location? Do you have access to the funds necessary?

2. *Stay the same.* No bar-related business stays exactly the same. Even though your bar's overall concept and clientele may stay the same, the promotions will have to change to match the current trends. If you decide to keep your bar the way it is, then you're saying that you've reached your goals in the way you serve your community. There's nothing wrong with enjoying success; just realize that you may have to change a little bit to remain successful.

3. *Franchise.* When you own a chain of bars, you're solely responsible for them. If you sell a franchise, the owner of each location is responsible for it. When considering this option, make sure your idea can succeed on a national or regional level. Talk to your lawyer and other experts in the industry before you decide to franchise.

4. *Sell.* Some entrepreneurs open a business and build its success with the idea of eventually selling it. These owners pour themselves into the promotion end of the business, drumming up big profits early and then selling the business based on those numbers.

president—what you can and what you can't do—was pretty educational and a little bit intimidating."

"I don't think it gets any bigger than getting the president of the United States into your nightclub," he says. "I don't think I could ever match that unless I get Queen Elizabeth to come over for the weekend."

Knowledge, experience, money, time, effort, rhyme, rhythm, reason, and a sound business plan are all you need to make it big in this sensational industry. Successful bars can and do exist. Will your bar be one of them?

If you follow the steps in this book, constantly check what you think is true against other advice and expertise, and get help from professionals in the field, you certainly can do it. Most of all, never lose sight of how lucky you are to be in a position to own a business—even if that luck was built by your own hard work. You live in a place and time where you can be your own boss and have a true shot at succeeding. How lucky is that? Many people wish they could do what you're about to do.

Congratulations, and go get 'em!

Appendix
Bar/Club Resources

They say you can never be too rich or too thin. While these could be argued, we believe you can never have too many resources. Therefore, we present for your consideration a wealth of sources for you to check into, check out, and harness for your own personal information blitz. These sources are tidbits, ideas to get you started on your research. They are by no means the only sources out there, and they should not be taken as the Ultimate Answer. We've done our research, but businesses—like customers—tend to move, change, fold, and expand. As we have repeatedly stressed, do your homework. Get out and start investigating.

Alcoholic Beverage Control Agencies

National Alcohol Beverage Control Association
4401 Ford Ave., #700
Alexandria, VA 22302
(703) 578-4200
nabca.org

Alabama Alcoholic Beverage Control Board
2715 Gunter Park Dr. W.
Montgomery, AL 36109
(334) 271-3840
abcboard.state.al.us

Alaska Department of Revenue
Alcoholic Beverage Control Board
5848 E. Tudor Rd.
Anchorage, AK 99507
(907) 269-0350
dps.state.ak.us/abc

Arizona Department of Liquor Licenses and Control
800 W. Washington, 5th Fl.
Phoenix, AZ 85007
(602) 542-5141
azliquor.gov

Arkansas Alcohol Beverage Control Administration Division
1515 W. Seventh St., #503
Little Rock, AR 72201
(501) 682-1105
arkansas.gov/dfa/abc_administration

California Department of Alcoholic Beverage Control
3927 Lennane Dr., #100
Sacramento, CA 95834
(916) 419-2500
abc.ca.gov

Colorado Department of Revenue
Liquor Enforcement Division
1881 Pierce St., #108A
Denver, CO 80214
(303) 205-2300
colorado.gov/revenue/liquor

Connecticut Department of Consumer Protection
Liquor Division, State Office Building
165 Capitol Ave.
Hartford, CT 06106
(860) 713-6200
ct.gov/dcp/cwp/view.asp?a=1623&q=273660

Delaware Alcoholic Beverage Control Commission
820 N. French St., 3rd Fl.
Wilmington, DE 19801
(302) 577-5222
date.delaware.gov/

District of Columbia Alcoholic Beverage Regulation Administration
941 N. Capitol St. NE, #7200
Washington, DC 20002
(202) 442-4423
abra.dc.gov

Florida Department of Professional Business Regulations
Division of Alcoholic Beverages & Tobacco
1940 N. Monroe St.
Tallahassee, FL 32399
(850) 487-1395
myflorida.com/dbpr/abt

Georgia Department of Revenue
Alcohol and Tobacco Division
P.O. Box 49728
Atlanta, GA 30359
(404) 417-4900
dor.ga.gov/alcohol/alc_forms.aspx

Hawaii Department of Liquor Control
711 Kapiolani Blvd., #600
Honolulu, HI 96813
(808) 768-7355
co.honolulu.hi.us/liq

Idaho State Liquor Dispensary
1349 E. Beechcroft Ct.
Boise, ID 83716
(208) 947-9400
liquor.idaho.gov/

Illinois Liquor Control Commission
100 W. Randolph St., #7801
Chicago, IL 60601
(312) 814-2206
state.il.us/lcc

▲

Indiana Alcoholic Beverage Commission
Indiana Government Center South, Room E-114
302 W. Washington St.
Indianapolis, IN 46204
(317) 232-2430
in.gov/atc

Iowa Alcoholic Beverages Division
1918 SE Hulsizer Ave.
Ankeny, IA 50021
(515) 281-7400
iowaabd.com

Kansas Department of Revenue
Division of Alcoholic Beverage Control
915 SW Harrison St., #214
Topeka, KS 66625-3512
(785) 296-7015
ksrevenue.org/abc.htm

Kentucky Department of Alcoholic Beverage Control
1003 Twilight Trail
Frankfort, KY 40601
(502) 564-4850
abc.ky.gov

Louisiana Office of Alcohol and Tobacco Control
8585 Archives Ave., #220
Baton Rouge, LA 70809
(225) 925-4041
atc.rev.state.la.us

Maine Bureau of Alcoholic Beverages & Lottery Operations
8 State House Station
Augusta, ME 04333
(207) 287-3721
state.me.us/dafs/bablo/index.shtml

State of Maryland, Comptroller of the Treasury
Alcohol and Tobacco Tax Division
80 Calvert St., #310
Annapolis, MD 21404
(410) 260-7131
compnet.comp.state.md.us/MATT_Regulatory_Division/Alcohol_and_Tobacco_Tax

Maryland Department of Liquor Control
16650 Crabbs Branch Wy.
Rockville, MD 20855
(240) 777-1900
montgomerycountymd.gov/dlc

Massachusetts Alcohol Beverages Control Commission
239 Causeway St.
Boston, MA 02114
(617) 727-3040
mass.gov/abcc

Michigan Liquor Control Commission
7150 Harris Dr.
P.O. Box 30005
Lansing, MI 48909
(866) 813-0011)
michigan.gov/dleg

Minnesota Department of Public Safety
Alcohol & Gambling Enforcement Division
444 Cedar St., #133
St. Paul, MN 55101
(651) 201-7500
dps.state.mn.us/alcgamb/alcgamb.aspx

Mississippi Office of Alcoholic Beverage Control
State Tax Commission
P.O. Box 540
Madison, MS 39310
(601) 856-1320
mstc.state.ms.us/abc/main.htm

Missouri Division of Alcohol and Tobacco Control
1738 E. Elm St., Lower Level, East Door
Jefferson City, MO 65101
(573) 751-2333
atc.dps.mo.gov/

Montana Department of Revenue, Liquor Division
P.O. Box 1712
Helena, MT 59604
(404) 444-6900
mt.gov/revenue/forbusinesses/alcohol.asp

Nebraska Liquor Control Commission
301 Centennial Mall S.
P.O. Box 95046
Lincoln, NE 68509
(402) 471-2571
lcc.ne.gov/

Nevada Department of Taxation
Liquor Division
1550 College Pkwy.
Carson City, NV 89706
(775) 684-2000
tax.state.nv.us

New Hampshire State Liquor Commission
50 Storrs St.
P.O. Box 503
Concord, NH 03302-0503
(603) 271-3521
nh.gov/liquor

New Jersey Department of Law and Public Safety
Division of Alcoholic Beverage Control
140 E. Front St., 5th Fl.
P.O. Box 087
Trenton, NJ 08625
(609) 984-2830
state.nj.us/lps/abc/index.html

New Mexico Regulation & Licensing Department
Alcohol and Gaming Division
2550 Cerrillos Rd., 2nd Fl.
Santa Fe, NM 87505
(505) 476-4875
rld.state.nm.us/agd

New York State Liquor Authority
Division of Alcoholic Beverage Control
80 S. Swan St., 9th Fl.
Albany, NY, 12210
(518) 474-3114
abc.state.ny.us

North Carolina Alcoholic Beverage Control Commission
4307 Mail Service Center
Raleigh, NC 27699-4307
(919) 779-0700
ncabc.com

North Dakota Office of the State Treasurer
Alcohol Beverage Control, State Capitol
600 E. Boulevard Ave.
Bismarck, ND 58505
(701) 328-2770
nd.gov/tax/alcohol/

Ohio Department of Commerce
Division of Liquor Control
6606 Tussing Rd.
Reynoldsburg, OH 43068
(614) 644-2556
com.ohio.gov/liqr

Oklahoma Alcoholic Beverage Laws Enforcement Commission
4545 N. Lincoln Blvd., #270
Oklahoma City, OK 73105
(405) 521-3484
ok.gov/able

Oregon Liquor Control Commission
9079 SE McLoughlin Blvd.
Milwaukee, OR 97222
(800) 452-6522
oregon.gov/OLCC/index.shtml

Pennsylvania Liquor Control Board
602 Northwest Office Bldg.
Harrisburg, PA 17124
(717) 783-7637
lcb.state.pa.us

Rhode Island Department of Business Regulation
Liquor Enforcement and Compliance
1511 Pontiac Ave.
Cranston, RI 02920
(401) 462-9506
dbr.ri.gov/divisions/commlicensing/liquor.php

▲

South Carolina Department of Revenue
Alcohol Beverage Licensing Section
301 Gervais St.
P.O. Box 125
Columbia, SC 29214
(803) 896-1970
sctax.org

South Dakota Department of Revenue & Regulation
Division of Special Taxes & Licensing
445 E. Capitol Ave.
Pierre, SD 57501
(605) 773-3311
state.sd.us/drr2/propspectax/alcohol/faq.htm

Tennessee Alcoholic Beverage Commission
226 Capitol Blvd.
Nashville, TN 37219
(615) 741-1602
state.tn.us/abc

Texas Alcoholic Beverage Commission
5806 Mesa Dr.
Austin, TX 78731
(512) 206-3333
tabc.state.tx.us

Utah Department of Alcoholic Beverage Control
1625 S. 900 W.
Salt Lake City, UT 84130
(801) 977-6800
alcbev.state.ut.us

Vermont Department of Liquor Control
State Office Bldg., 13 Green Mountain Dr., Drawer #20
Montpelier, VT 05620
(802) 828-2345
state.vt.us/dlc

Virginia Department of Alcoholic Beverage Control
P.O. Box 27491
Richmond, VA 23261
(804) 213-4400
abc.state.va.us

Washington State Liquor Control Board
3000 Pacific Ave. SE
Olympia, WA 98504-3080
(360) 664-1600
liq.wa.gov

West Virginia Alcohol Beverage Control Administration
322 70th St. SE
Charleston, WV 25304
(304) 558-2481
wvabca.com

Wisconsin Department of Revenue
2135 Rimrock Rd.
Madison, WI 53713
(608) 266-2772
dor.state.wi.us

Wyoming Liquor Commission
1520 E. Fifth St.
Cheyenne, WY 82002
(307) 777-7231
revenue.state.wy.us

Associations

Distilled Spirits Council of the United States
1250 Eye St. NW, #400
Washington, DC 20005
(202) 628-3544
discus.org

National Bar & Restaurant Management Association
307 W. Jackson Ave.
Oxford, MS 38655
(662) 236-5510

National Restaurant Association
1200 17th St. NW
Washington, DC 20036
(202) 331-5900
restaurant.org

Books

Complete World Bartender Guide, Bob Sennett, Editor, Bantam Books

The Disgusting Practice of Bartender Theft, Bob Johnson, available at bobthe
barguy.com

How to Open and Run a Successful Restaurant, Christopher Egerton-Thomas,
John Wiley & Sons

Running a Successful Bar, Bob Johnson, (also includes *The 49 Ways Bartenders
Steal*), available at bobthebarguy.com

The Upstart Guide to Owning and Managing a Bar or Tavern, Roy S. Alonzo,
Kaplan Publishing

Education

Bob Johnson's School of Bar Management
P.O. Box 1050
Clearwater, SC 29822
(800) 447-4384
bobthebarguy.com

General Resources

Beer Institute
122 C St. NW, #350
Washington, DC 20001
(202) 737-2337
beerinstitute.org

Liquor Control Systems
Auper Electronic Controls Inc.
901 Michelin
Laval, QB, CAN H7L-5B6
(450) 663-1993
auper.com

Automatic Bar Controls Inc./Wunder-Bar
790 Eubanks Dr.
Vacaville, CA 95688
(800) 722-6738
wunderbar.com

Magnuson Industries/Posi-Pour
(800) 435-2816
posi-pour.com

Online Resources

Alcohol and Tobacco Tax and Trade Bureau
U.S. Dept of the Treasury
ttb.gov

The Beverage Information Group
17 High St., 2nd Fl.
Norwalk, CT 06851
(203) 855-8499
beveragenet.net

Publications

Bartender Magazine
P.O. Box 158
Liberty Corner, NJ 07938
(908) 766-6006
bartender.com

Brew Your Own
5515 Main St.
Manchester Center, VT 05254
byo.com

Mobile Beat—The Mobile Entertainer's Magazine
P.O. Box 42365
Urbandale, IA 50322
(515) 986-3300,
mobilebeat.com

Nightclub & Bar
307 W. Jackson Ave.
Oxford, MS 38655
(662) 236-5510
nightclub.com

Restaurant Business
restaurantbiz.com

Wine Business Monthly
110 W. Napa St.
Sonoma, CA 95476
(707) 939-0822
winebusiness.com

Wine Spectator
winespectator.com

Successful Bar/Club Owners

Bob Brenlin
Fiddler's Inn
9219 35th St. NE
Seattle, WA 98115
(206) 525-0752

R.C. Colvin
Round Table Bar & Grill
3024 N. U.S. Hwy. 31
Niles, MI 49120
(269) 683-9738

Gerry Kelly
The Fifth
1045 Fifth St.
Miami Beach, FL 33139
(305) 538-9898
thefifth.com

Ron Newman
Baja Sharkeez (corporate office)
703 Pier Ave., Ste. B-815
Hermosa Beach, CA 90254
(310) 420-9117

Glossary

Alcoholic Beverage Control (ABC) agencies: state and county government licensing agencies that issue liquor licenses and beer and wine licenses.

Alcohol and Tobacco Tax and Trade Bureau (TTB): the federal regulating agency for any establishment with a liquor license.

Average guest check: how much the average customer spends at a bar or restaurant.

Back bar: the shelves and cabinets behind the bar that face the customers; this area usually displays premium liquor bottles.

Back of the house: the kitchen, office, and storage areas of a bar; only employees are allowed in these areas.

Barback: An employee who keeps the bar stocked, clean, and user-friendly for the bartender.

Call-brand drinks: midpriced drinks, between well-brand drinks and premium-brand drinks.

Food-cost percentage: the percentage of food sales that a bar spends on ingredients.

Front bar: area at a bar where guests sit on stools or chairs, including the bar top and bar front.

Front of the house: the public area of the bar where the guests eat, drink, and mingle.

Labor-cost percentage: the percentage of your sales that you spend on your payroll expenses.

Nonperformance-based entertainment: entertainment options that only require equipment, as opposed to entertainers.

Par: the amount of backup bottles that are needed behind the bar to supply one business day.

Performance-based entertainment: entertainment options that require people to perform, such as musicians, comedians, or DJs.

Performing rights associations: agencies responsible for monitoring and dispensing royalties to musicians and songwriters.

Pour-cost percentage: the percentage of liquor sales that a bar spends on liquor-related costs.

Premium-brand drinks: the highest-priced drinks that use the best liquor in the bar; *see top shelf.*

Top shelf: the highest-priced liquor, usually placed on the highest shelves behind the bar.

Under bar: the area behind the bar that customers can't see; this is the area where the bartender does most of his or her work.

Upselling: encouraging your customers to order a call or premium brand instead of a well drink.

Well-brand drinks: the lowest-priced drinks, usually served when a customer orders a generic drink, such as "rum and coke" or "scotch and water"; located in a well rack behind the bar.

Index